THE COMPLETE KETO DIET FOR UK BEGINNERS

1000 Delicous, Quick and Easy Ketogenic Recipes and 4-Week Meal Plan for Everyone Full Colour Version

GRACE J. SMALLEY

Copyright© 2022 Grace J. Smalley By Rights Reserved

This book is copyright protected. It is only for personal use. You cannot amend, distribute, sell, use, quote or paraphrase any part of the content within this book, without the consent of the author or publisher.

Under no circumstances will any blame or legal responsibility be held against the publisher, or author, for any damages, reparation, or monetary loss due to the information contained within this book, either directly or indirectly.

Disclaimer Notice:

Please note the information contained within this document is for educational and entertainment purposes only. All effort has been executed to present accurate, up to date, reliable, complete information. No warranties of any kind are declared or implied. Readers acknowledge that the author is not engaged in the rendering of legal, financial, medical or professional advice. The content within this book has been derived from various sources. Please consult a licensed professional before attempting any techniques outlined in this book.

By reading this document, the reader agrees that under no circumstances is the author responsible for any losses, direct or indirect, that are incurred as a result of the use of the information contained within this document, including, but not limited to, errors, omissions, or inaccuracies.

Table of Contents

Introduction	1
Chapter 1	
Basics of Keto Diet	2
What is Ketogenic Diet?	3
Proven Benefits of Keto Diet	3
The Best Tips to Get into Ketosis	4
Chapter 2	
28-Day Meal Plan	7
Week 1	8
Week 2	10
Week 3	12
Week 4	14
Chapter 3	
Breakfast	16
Breakfast Coconut Porridge	17
Egg Butter	17
Flax Meal Porridge	18
Scrambled Pancake Hash	18
Morning Time Sausages	19
Chicken Muffins	19
Spiced Eggs	20
Olives and Eggs Mix	20
Cheesy Frittata	21
Herbed Omelet	21
Eggs Ramekins	22
Paprika Omelet with Goat Cheese	22
Cheese Mix	23
Chili Eggs	23
Cheese Muffins	24
Dilly Boiled Eggs with Avocado	24
Greek-Style Frittata with Herbs	24
Chapter 4	
Snacks & Appetizers	25
Spicy Mango Okra	26
Parsley & Garlic Flavored Potatoes	26
Turmeric & Garlic Roasted Carrots	27
Paprika Chips	27
Bacon & Veggie Mash	28
Coconut Cheese Sticks	28
Sprouts Wraps	29
Broccoli Puree	29
Zucchini Chips	30
Chives and Spinach	30
Chili Zucchini Tots	31
Ham Cheese Egg Cups	31
Broccoli Hash Brown	32
Cheese Rounds	32
Bacon Avocado Wraps	33
Saucy and Spicy Spareribs	33
Parm Bites	34
Taco Chicken Wings	34
Ham and Avocado Stuffed Eggs	35

Two Cheese and Prosciutto Balls	35
Stuffed Mini Peppers	35

Chapter 5
Chicken and Poultry — 36

Chicken with Sauce, Vegetables & Rice	37
Philly Chicken Cheesesteak Stromboli	37
Prawn Paste Chicken Wings	37
Old Bay Crispy Chicken Wings	37
Jerk-Style Chicken Wings	38
Parmesan and Dill Chicken	38
Ginger and Coconut Chicken	38
Tomato Chicken Mix	38
Spinach Chicken Wings	39
Asparagus Chicken	39
Buttery Chicken Wings	39
Cream Cheese Chicken Mix	39
Nutmeg Chicken Fillets	39
Taco Chicken	39
Chicken Thighs with Kalamata Olives	40
Sunday Chicken Bake	40
Primavera Stuffed Turkey Fillets	40
Teriyaki Turkey Bowls	40
Keto TSO Chicken	41
Chicken with Asparagus and Zucchini	41
Greek-Style Chicken Mélange	41
Mediterranean Roasted Chicken with Aromatics	41

Chapter 6
Beef, Lamb and Pork — 42

Sausage Balls	43
Keto Breakfast Bacon	43
Pork Breakfast Sticks	43
Pork and Garlic Sauce	43
Creamy Cheesy Bacon Dip	44
Chili Pork	44
Cilantro Beef Meatballs	44
Beef Under Cabbage Blanket	44
Basil Pork	45
Coconut Beef Steak	45
Beef & Potato	45
Baked Beef Bowl	45
Beef Roast	45
Beef & Mushrooms	45
Hearty Pork Stew	46
Fast Mongolian Beef	46
Rich Bacon and Pork Omelet	46
Saucy Pork Cutlets	47
Simple and Delicious Chili Con Carne	47

Chapter 7
Fish and Seafood — 48

Kataifi-Wrapped Shrimp with Lemon Garlic Butter	49
Fish Taco	49
Grilled Barramundi with Lemon Butter	49
Ginger Cod	50
Paprika Tilapia	50
Butter Crab Muffins	50
Cranberry Cod	50
Shrimp Skewers	51
Cod Fish Teriyaki with Oysters, Mushrooms & Veggies	51
Stevia Cod	51
Onion Shrimps	51
Balsamic Tilapia	52
Crunchy Red Fish	52

Chapter 8
Vegetarian Recipes — 53

Croissant Mushroom & Egg	54
Mushroom, Onion and Feta Frittata	54
Lemon Asparagus	54
Bacon, Lettuce, Tempeh & Tomato Sandwiches	54
Curried Cauliflower Florets	55
Mustard Garlic Asparagus	55
Nutmeg Okra	55
Parsnip Fries	55
Feta Peppers	55
Sesame Fennel	55
Swiss Chard Patties	56
Bacon Asparagus	56
Snap Peas Mash	56

Chapter 9
Desserts and Staples — 57

Country-Style Coconut & Macadamia Cookies	58
Almond Butter Cookies	58
Chocolate Raspberry Cake	58
Lemon Zucchini Bread	58
Orange Muffins	59
Tender Macadamia Bars	59
Lemon Pie	59
Raisin Muffins	59
Cinnamon Zucchini Bread	60
Cream Cheese Scones	60
Bread Pudding with Sultanas	60
Berry Pie	60
Vanilla Scones	61
Poppy Seeds Muffins	61
Almond Pie	61

Appendix 1 Measurement Conversion Chart — 62
Appendix 2 The Dirty Dozen and Clean Fifteen — 63
Appendix 3 Index — 64

Introduction

My life was going well, and I was living like a regular person. A few years ago I started gaining weight out of thin air. I felt like everything I ate was converting into fat and staying in my body. Then I started dieting. I have tried many diets in my life, I used to lose some pounds then again gained weight. Because of dieting, my body started to feel tired and I could not exercise. Not exercising increased my weight more than it was before.

Finally, a friend of mine introduced me to the keto diet. This diet was very helpful for me and I lost weight faster. Now I can exercise and don't have that tiredness in my body. To follow a keto diet you have to understand how it works.

The ketogenic diet is basically a low-carb and protein-focused diet. Instead of consuming carbohydrates, you have to consume measured protein and fat. Avoiding carbs puts the human body into a metabolic state called ketosis and this is where the name came from.

A ketogenic diet contains 80%-60% fat, 10%-30% protein, and 5%-10% carbohydrate. This diet decreases the appetite and turns fat and protein into glucose. This is how the ketogenic diet works.

The best thing about this diet is it restores energy and does not make the person weak. Getting weak during the process is one of the main reasons for an unsuccessful diet.

No wonder why a ketogenic diet is so helpful in losing weight and living a healthy life. The problem is people do not have enough guidelines for following a keto diet. This is why I wrote this book. I do not want people to face the problems I faced while following a ketogenic diet.

There are different types of keto diets explained in this diet book so you can follow whichever suits you. It has different delicious dishes that will help you keep your mind happy with tasty food. If you do not have enough information about the keto diet, you can follow this diet book as a guideline.

This diet book has all kinds of recipes that include vegetables, fish, meat, egg, chicken, beef, and even pork. You can find any recipe and follow it without any confusion. The calorie count is given properly which will help you count how much you consumed. All the recipes are personally tasted and you can try them without any worries.

This is a perfect diet book for beginners, it has a lot of information about different types of the keto diet. It will help you learn and explore more about dieting.

In the end, I want to thank everyone for reading my book at this moment. I hope this diet book will help you lose weight and reach your goal. If you find it helpful then you can share this diet book with your loved ones who are also interested in losing weight. They will be grateful to you for the diet book. Live a healthy and great life.

Chapter 1
Basics of Keto Diet

What is Ketogenic Diet?

A ketogenic diet, also known as the "keto diet," is a high-fat, low-carbohydrate diet that has been shown to be effective for weight loss and other health benefits. The goal of the diet is to get the body into a state of ketosis, in which it is using fat, rather than carbohydrates, as its primary source of energy.

On a ketogenic diet, the majority of calories come from fat, with a moderate amount of protein and a very low intake of carbohydrates. The typical macronutrient breakdown is 70-80% fat, 15-25% protein, and 5-10% carbohydrates.

Proven Benefits of Keto Diet

A keto diet leads to weight loss.

There is some evidence to suggest that a ketogenic diet may be effective for weight loss. The high-fat, low-carbohydrate nature of the diet may lead to weight loss due to several factors, including:

Reduced calorie intake: When following a ketogenic diet, it is often easier to control calorie intake because the high-fat content of the diet can help reduce hunger and cravings.

Increased fat burning: The body may burn more fat for energy on a ketogenic diet, as it is using fat, rather than carbohydrates, as its primary fuel source.

Improved blood sugar control: The low-carbohydrate nature of the diet may help improve blood sugar control and reduce the risk of insulin resistance, which is a risk factor for weight gain.

Mental clarity and better concentration.

People report improved mental clarity and better concentration while following a ketogenic diet. This may be due to several factors, including:

Improved blood sugar control: The low-carbohydrate nature of the diet may help improve blood sugar control,

which can lead to more stable energy levels and better concentration.

Increased ketones: When the body is in a state of ketosis, it produces ketones, which are an alternative source of energy for the brain. Some people may find that the increased production of ketones leads to improved mental clarity and focus.

Reduced inflammation: A ketogenic diet may help reduce inflammation in the body, which can have a positive impact on brain health and cognitive function.

IMPROVED BLOOD SUGAR CONTROL

There is evidence to suggest that the ketogenic diet may help improve blood sugar control and reduce the risk of insulin resistance, which is a risk factor for type 2 diabetes. The low-carbohydrate nature of the diet may lead to improved blood sugar control in several ways:

Reduced carbohydrate intake: By limiting carbohydrate intake, the ketogenic diet may help reduce the risk of blood sugar spikes after meals.

Increased fat burning: The body may burn more fat for energy on a ketogenic diet, which can lead to improved insulin sensitivity and better blood sugar control.

Increased ketones: When the body is in a state of ketosis, it produces ketones, which are an alternative source of energy for the body. Some research suggests that ketones may have a positive impact on blood sugar control and insulin sensitivity.

The Best Tips to Get into Ketosis

Ketosis is a metabolic state in which the body burns fat, rather than carbohydrates, as its primary source of energy. This occurs when the body does not have enough carbohydrates available to use for energy, so it begins to break down stored fat into molecules called ketones, which can be used for energy.

The ketogenic diet, also known as the "keto diet," is a high-fat, low-carbohydrate diet that is designed to get the body into a state of ketosis. When following this diet, the majority of calories come from fat, with a moderate amount of protein and a very low intake of carbohydrates. The typical macronutrient breakdown is 70-80% fat, 15-25% protein, and 5-10% carbohydrates.

Ketosis can be measured through various methods, including urine testing, blood testing, and breath testing.

Increase your healthy fat intake

Increasing your intake of healthy fats is one way to help you get into a state of ketosis when following a ketogenic diet. To increase your intake of healthy fats on a ketogenic diet, you can incorporate foods such as:

Avocado: This fruit is high in monounsaturated fats and can be added to salads, sandwiches, or used as a spread.

Nuts and seeds: Nuts and seeds, such as almonds, walnuts, and chia seeds, are high in healthy fats and can be eaten as a snack or added to meals.

Olive oil: This oil is high in monounsaturated fats and can be used for cooking or as a dressing for salads.

Coconut oil: This oil is high in medium-chain triglycerides (MCTs) and can be used for cooking or added to beverages as an energy boost.

Grass-fed butter: This type of butter is high in healthy fats and can be used for cooking or added to foods as a condiment.

TRY ANCIENT PRACTICE OF INTERMITTENT FASTING

Intermittent fasting is an ancient practice that involves periods of voluntary abstinence from food and drink. There are several different intermittent fasting patterns, but one common approach is to fast for a certain number of hours each day or to have one or two non-consecutive days each week when you eat very little or nothing at all.

Intermittent fasting may help increase ketone production and promote ketosis by limiting the availability of carbohydrates and increasing the breakdown of fat for energy.

VARIETY IS THE KEY

Eating a variety of foods is important for overall health and can also be helpful when following a ketogenic diet.

Incorporating a variety of foods into your diet can help ensure that you are getting a wide range of nutrients and can also help make the diet more enjoyable. Some tips for adding variety to your ketogenic diet include:

Choose a variety of protein sources: Include a variety of protein sources, such as poultry, fish, eggs, nuts, and seeds, to ensure that you are getting a wide range of nutrients.

Include a variety of vegetables: Choose a variety of vegetables, including leafy greens, cruciferous vegetables, and colorful produce, to add nutrients and flavor to your diet.

Experiment with different fats: While it's important to include healthy fats in your diet, it's also a good idea to try different types of fats, such as olive oil, avocado, and nuts, to add flavor and variety.

Don't forget about carbohydrates: While the ketogenic diet is low in carbohydrates, it's still important to include a variety of carbohydrate sources, such as non-starchy vegetables and small amounts of whole grains, to ensure that you are getting a wide range of nutrients.

By incorporating a variety of foods into your diet, you can help ensure that you are getting all of the nutrients your body needs and can make the diet more enjoyable.

USE MCT OIL.

MCT oil is a type of oil that is high in medium-chain triglycerides (MCTs), a type of fat that is easily digestible and quickly converted into energy by the liver. MCT oil has gained popularity as a supplement for people following a ketogenic diet, also known as the "keto diet," due to its potential to help increase ketone production and promote ketosis.

The ketogenic diet is a high-fat, low-carbohydrate diet that is designed to get the body into a state of ketosis, in which it is using fat, rather than carbohydrates, as its primary source of energy. When the body is in a state of ketosis, it breaks down stored fat into molecules called ketones, which can be used for energy.

Some research suggests that MCT oil may help increase ketone production and promote ketosis by providing an alternative source of energy for the body. However, it is important to note that MCT oil may not be suitable for everyone and may cause side effects, such as digestive discomfort and diarrhea, in some people. It's a good idea to start with a small dosage and gradually increase it to avoid these side effects.

CONSUME PROTEIN-RICH FOODS

Incorporating protein-rich foods into a ketogenic diet, also known as the "keto diet," can be helpful for maintaining muscle mass and supporting overall health.
Protein is an important nutrient that plays a number of roles in the body, including building and repairing tissues, making enzymes and hormones, and supporting immune function. When following a ketogenic diet, it is important to consume enough protein to meet your needs and support your goals.

Some protein-rich foods that can be included in a ketogenic diet include:

Meat: Choose lean cuts of meat, such as chicken, turkey, and beef, to add protein to your diet.

Fish: Fish, such as salmon and tuna, is a good source of protein and is also high in omega-3 fatty acids, which are important for heart health.

Eggs: Eggs are a good source of protein and can be included in a variety of dishes, such as omelets and frittatas.

Nuts and seeds: Nuts and seeds, such as almonds, walnuts, and chia seeds, are high in protein and can be eaten as a snack or added to meals.

Dairy products: Dairy products, such as milk, cheese, and yogurt, are good sources of protein, but it's important to choose low-carb options when following a ketogenic diet.

By incorporating protein-rich foods into your diet, you can help support muscle mass and overall health while following a ketogenic diet.

Do not underestimate the importance of the physical activity.

Physical activity can be helpful for getting into a state of ketosis when following a ketogenic diet. Physical activity can help promote ketosis by increasing the demand for energy and encouraging the body to use stored fat for fuel. In addition, regular physical activity has a number of other health benefits, including improving cardiovascular health, strengthening bones and muscles, and reducing the risk of chronic diseases.

Chapter 2
28-Day Meal Plan

Week 1

Here is the following first week's meal plan for the keto diet. Try to follow the plan thoroughly to start getting the benefits of a keto diet.

Meal Plan	Breakfast	Snack	Lunch	Dinner	Snack
Day-1	Breakfast Coconut Porridge	Spicy Mango Okra (2 servings)	Prawn Paste Chicken Wings	Pork and Garlic Sauce	Paprika Chips (2 servings)
	Calories: 169 | Total Fat: 18.2g | Carbs: 9.3g | Protein: 4.2g	Calories: 35 | Total Fat: 0.11g | Carbs: 7.7g | Protein: 2.27g	Calories: 287 | Total Fat: 10.2g | Carbs: 8.6g | Protein: 15.4g	Calories: 284 | Fat: 12g | Fiber: 4g | Carbs: 6g | Protein: 19g	Calories: 62 | Total Fat: 6.5g | Carbs: 41.5g | Protein: 5.3g
Day-2	Egg Butter	Bacon & Veggie Mash (2 servings)	Creamy Cheesy Bacon Dip	Cranberry Cod	Coconut Cheese Sticks
	Calories: 164 | Total Fat: 8.5g | Carbs: 2.67g | Protein: 3g	Calories: 42 | Total Fat: 8.3g | Carbs: 9.5g | Protein: 16.2g	Calories: 271 | Fat: 22.5g | Fiber: 0g | Carbs: 1g | Protein: 15.6g	Calories: 289 | Total Fat: 9.2g | Carbs: 8.3g | Protein: 14.3g	Calories: 184 | Fat: 14.2g | Fiber: 0.7g | Carbs: 2.1g | Protein: 12.5g
Day-3	Scrambled Pancake Hash	Raisin Muffins	Fish Taco	Baked Beef Bowl	Spicy Mango Okra
	Calories: 178 | Total Fat: 13.3g | Carbs: 10.7g | Protein: 4.4g	Calories: 560 | Total Fat: 28.3g | Carbs: 73.4g | Protein: 7.9g	Calories: 302 | Total Fat: 9.2g | Carbs: 8.7g | Protein: 15.2g	Calories: 446 | Fat: 15.5g | Fiber: 1.5g | Carbs: 2.9g | Protein: 69.4g	Calories: 35 | Total Fat: 0.11g | Carbs: 7.7g | Protein: 2.27g
Day-4	Flax Meal Porridge	Berry Pie	Parsnip Fries	Hearty Pork Stew	Berry Pie
	Calories: 298 | Total Fat: 26.7g | Carbs: 13.3 g | Protein: 6.2g	Calories: 182 | Fat: 12g | Fiber: 1g | Carbs: 6g | Protein: 5g	Calories: 262g | Total Fat: 11.3g | Carbs: 10.4g | Protein: 7.2g	Calories: 332 | Fat: 14.7g | Carbs: 3.9g | Protein: 41g | Fiber: 0.8g	Calories: 182 | Fat: 12g | Fiber: 1g | Carbs: 6g | Protein: 5g
Day-5	Morning Time Sausages	Vanilla Scones	Beef & Mushrooms	Saucy Pork Cutlets	Vanilla Scones

		Calories: 156 | Total Fat: 7.5g | Carbs: 1.3g | Protein: 20.2g	Calories: 104 | Fat: 4.1g | Fiber: 8.1g | Carbs: 14g | Protein: 3g	Calories: 296 | Total Fat: 12.4g | Carbs: 11.3g | Protein: 16.2g	Calories: 369 | Fat: 20.6g | Carbs: 1.1g | Protein: 40.1g | Fiber: 0.1g	Calories: 104 | Fat: 4.1g | Fiber: 8.1g | Carbs: 14g | Protein: 3g
Day-6	Chicken Muffins	Poppy Seeds Muffins	Stevia Cod	Beef Roast	Poppy Seeds Muffins
	Calories: 291 | Fat: 20.6g | Fiber: 1.3g | Carbs: 2.7g | Protein: 23.9g	Calories: 239 | Fat: 17.7g | Fiber: 9.8g | Carbs: 17.1g | Protein: 4.6g	Calories: 267 | Fat: 18g | Fiber: 2g | Carbs: 5g | Protein: 20g	Calories: 435 | Fat: 15.1g | Fiber: 0.7g | Carbs: 1.3g | Protein: 69.1g	Calories: 239 | Fat: 17.7g | Fiber: 9.8g | Carbs: 17.1g | Protein: 4.6g
Day-7	Spiced Eggs	Almond Pie (2 servings)	Onion Shrimps	Old Bay Crispy Chicken Wings	Almond Pie (2 servings)
	Calories: 130 fat 9g | Fiber: 0.4g | Carbs: 1.3g | Protein: 11.2g	Calories: 89 | Fat: 7.9g | Fiber: 0.9g | Carbs: 2g | Protein: 2g	Calories: 185 | Fat: 2.8g | Fiber: 0.1g | Carbs: 3g | Protein: 34.5g	Calories: 302 | Total Fat: 11.5g | Carbs: 9.6g | Protein: 16.3g	Calories: 89 | Fat: 7.9g | Fiber: 0.9g | Carbs: 2g | Protein: 2g

Week 2

Here is the following second week's meal plan for a keto diet. It's the second stage of the 4 weeks meal plan that you must take into account carefully.

Meal Plan	Breakfast	Snack	Lunch	Dinner	Snack
Day-1	Eggs Ramekins	Paprika Chips (2 servings)	Prawn Paste Chicken Wings	Pork and Garlic Sauce	Parm Bites
	Calories: 144 | Fat: 8g | Fiber: 4.5g | Carbs: 9.1g | Protein: 8.8g	Calories: 62 | Total Fat: 6.5g | Carbs: 41.5g | Protein: 5.3g	Calories: 287 | Total Fat: 10.2g | Carbs: 8.6g | Protein: 15.4g	Calories: 284 | Fat: 12g | Fiber: 4g | Carbs: 6g | Protein: 19g	Calories: 136 | Fat: 6.2g | Fiber: 7.7g | Carbs: 13.7g | Protein: 9.4g
Day-2	Paprika Omelet with Goat Cheese	Parm Bites	Creamy Cheesy Bacon Dip	Cranberry Cod	Spicy Mango Okra (2 servings)
	Calories: 287 | Fat: 22.6g | Carbs: 1.3g | Protein: 19.8g | Fiber: 0g	Calories: 136 | Fat: 6.2g | Fiber: 7.7g | Carbs: 13.7g | Protein: 9.4g	Calories: 271 | Fat: 22.5g | Fiber: 0g | Carbs: 1g | Protein: 15.6g	Calories: 289 | Total Fat: 9.2g | Carbs: 8.3g | Protein: 14.3g	Calories: 35 | Total Fat: 0.11g | Carbs: 7.7g | Protein: 2.27g
Day-3	Cheese Mix	Parm Bites	Fish Taco	Baked Beef Bowl	Taco Chicken Wings
	Calories: 209 | Fat: 18.7g | Fiber: 0.9g | Carbs: 2.8g | Protein: 2.9g	Calories: 136 | Fat: 6.2g | Fiber: 7.7g | Carbs: 13.7g | Protein: 9.4g	Calories: 302 | Total Fat: 9.2g | Carbs: 8.7g | Protein: 15.2g	Calories: 446 | Fat: 15.5g | Fiber: 1.5g | Carbs: 2.9g | Protein: 69.4g	Calories: 293 | Fat: 12.1g | Carbs: 3.4g | Protein: 40.6g | Fiber: 0.9g
Day-4	Chili Eggs (2 servings)	Stuffed Mini Peppers	Creamy Cheesy Bacon Dip	Ginger Cod	Stuffed Mini Peppers
	Calories: 64 | Fat: 4.5g | Fiber: 0.1g | Carbs: 0.4g | Protein: 5.6g	Calories: 207 | Fat: 10.2g | Carbs: 6.8g | Protein: 19.7g | Fiber: 1.6g	Calories: 271 | Fat: 22.5g | Fiber: 0g | Carbs: 1g | Protein: 15.6g	Calories: 183 | Fat: 8.5g | Fiber: 0.7g | Carbs: 1.4g | Protein: 25.6g	Calories: 207 | Fat: 10.2g | Carbs: 6.8g | Protein: 19.7g | Fiber: 1.6g

Day-5	Chili Eggs (2 servings)	Broccoli Puree	Beef & Mushrooms	Saucy Pork Cutlets	Broccoli Puree
	Calories: 64 | Fat: 4.5g | Fiber: 0.1g | Carbs: 0.4g | Protein: 5.6g	Calories: 94 | Fat: 6.6g | Fiber: 3g | Carbs: 7.7g | Protein: 3.3g	Calories: 296 | Total Fat: 12.4g | Carbs: 11.3g | Protein: 16.2g	Calories: 369 | Fat: 20.6g | Carbs: 1.1g | Protein: 40.1g | Fiber: 0.1g	Calories: 94 | Fat: 6.6g | Fiber: 3g | Carbs: 7.7g | Protein: 3.3g
Day-6	Cheese Muffins	Zucchini Chips	Stevia Cod	Beef Roast	Chili Zucchini Tots
	Calories: 110 | Fat: 7.1g | Fiber: 1.1g | Carbs: 2g | Protein: 9.5g	Calories: 120 | Fat: 4g | Fiber: 2g | Carbs: 3g | Protein: 5g	Calories: 267 | Fat: 18g | Fiber: 2g | Carbs: 5g | Protein: 20g	Calories: 435 | Fat: 15.1g | Fiber: 0.7g | Carbs: 1.3g | Protein: 69.1g	Calories: 122 | Fat: 7.4g | Fiber: 3.7g | Carbs: 7.3g | Protein: 7.2g
Day-7	Dilly Boiled Eggs with Avocado	Cheese Rounds	Shrimp Skewers	Old Bay Crispy Chicken Wings	Parm Bites
	Calories: 222 | Fat: 17.6g | Carbs: 5.7g | Protein: 12.2g | Fiber: 3.9g	Calories: 114 | Fat: 9.4g | Fiber: 0g | Carbs: 0.4g | Protein: 7g	Calories: 223 | Fat: 14.9g | Fiber: 3.1g | Carbs: 5.5g | Protein: 17.4g	Calories: 302 | Total Fat: 11.5g | Carbs: 9.6g | Protein: 16.3g	Calories: 136 | Fat: 6.2g | Fiber: 7.7g | Carbs: 13.7g | Protein: 9.4g

Week 3

Here is the following third week's meal plan for a keto diet. In this stage, you already got the result of the previous two weeks' diet plan. So, follow this third stage of the meal plan completely to get a better result.

Meal Plan	Breakfast	Snack	Lunch	Dinner	Snack
Day-1	Olives and Eggs Mix	Lemon Zucchini Bread	Cilantro Beef Meatballs	Pork and Garlic Sauce	Paprika Chips (2 servings)
	Calories: 240 | Fat: 14g | Fiber: 3g | Carbs: 5g | Protein: 8g	Calories: 143 | Fat: 11g | Fiber: 1g | Carbs: 3g | Protein: 3g	Calories: 180 | Fat: 13g | Fiber: 0.8g | Carbs: 2.1g | Protein: 13.8g	Calories: 284 | Fat: 12g | Fiber: 4g | Carbs: 6g | Protein: 19g	Calories: 62 | Total Fat: 6.5g | Carbs: 41.5g | Protein: 5.3g
Day-2	Egg Butter	Spicy Mango Okra	Creamy Cheesy Bacon Dip	Cranberry Cod	Bread Pudding with Sultanas
	Calories: 164 | Total Fat: 8.5g | Carbs: 2.67g | Protein: 3g	Calories: 35 | Total Fat: 0.11g | Carbs: 7.7g | Protein: 2.27g	Calories: 271 | Fat: 22.5g | Fiber: 0g | Carbs: 1g | Protein: 15.6g	Calories: 289 | Total Fat: 9.2g | Carbs: 8.3g | Protein: 14.3g	Calories: 283 | Total Fat: 4.7g | Carbs: 51.4g | Protein: 8.3g
Day-3	Scrambled Pancake Hash	Orange Muffins	Coconut Beef Steak	Shrimp Skewers	Lemon Zucchini Bread
	Calories: 178 | Total Fat: 13.3g | Carbs: 10.7g | Protein: 4.4g	Calories: 119 | Fat: 7.1g | Fiber: 3.4g | Carbs: 6.2g | Protein: 7.5g	Calories: 509 | Fat: 24.3g | Fiber: 0g | Carbs: 0g | Protein: 68.8g	Calories: 223 | Fat: 14.9g | Fiber: 3.1g | Carbs: 5.5g | Protein: 17.4g	Calories: 143 | Fat: 11g | Fiber: 1g | Carbs: 3g | Protein: 3g
Day-4	Cheesy Frittata	Tender Macadamia Bars	Parsnip Fries	Hearty Pork Stew	Vanilla Scones (2 servings)
	Calories: 231 | Fat: 11g | Fiber: 3g | Carbs: 5g | Protein: 8g	Calories: 158 | Fat: 10.4g | Fiber: 7.7g | Carbs: 13.1g | Protein: 4g	Calories: 262g | Total Fat: 11.3g | Carbs: 10.4g | Protein: 7.2g	Calories: 332 | Fat: 14.7g | Carbs: 3.9g | Protein: 41g | Fiber: 0.8g	Calories: 104 | Fat: 4.1g | Fiber: 8.1g | Carbs: 14g | Protein: 3g
Day-5	Morning Time Sausages	Lemon Pie	Beef & Mushrooms	Saucy Pork Cutlets	Poppy Seeds Muffins

	Calories: 156 | Total Fat: 7.5g | Carbs: 1.3g | Protein: 20.2g	Calories: 212 | Fat: 15g | Fiber: 2g | Carbs: 6g | Protein: 4g	Calories: 296 | Total Fat: 12.4g | Carbs: 11.3g | Protein: 16.2g	Calories: 369 | Fat: 20.6g | Carbs: 1.1g | Protein: 40.1g | Fiber: 0.1g	Calories: 239 | Fat: 17.7g | Fiber: 9.8g | Carbs: 17.1g | Protein: 4.6g
Day-6	Chicken Muffins	Cream Cheese Scones	Stevia Cod	Beef Roast	Chocolate Raspberry Cake
	Calories: 291 | Fat: 20.6g | Fiber: 1.3g | Carbs: 2.7g | Protein: 23.9g	Calories: 217 | Fat: 19.6g | Fiber: 3.4g | Carbs: 7.4g | Protein: 6.6g	Calories: 267 | Fat: 18g | Fiber: 2g | Carbs: 5g | Protein: 20g	Calories: 435 | Fat: 15.1g | Fiber: 0.7g | Carbs: 1.3g | Protein: 69.1g	Calories: 331 | Total Fat: 14.9g | Carbs: 47.6g | Protein: 26.9g
Day-7	Herbed Omelet	Bread Pudding with Sultanas	Beef & Potato	Stevia Cod	Country-Style Coconut & Macadamia Cookies
	Calories: 232 | Fat: 12g | Fiber: 4g | Carbs: 5g | Protein: 7g	Calories: 283 | Total Fat: 4.7g | Carbs: 51.4g | Protein: 8.3g	Calories: 296 | Total Fat: 12.2g | Carbs: 11.8g | Protein: 16.3g	Calories: 267 | Fat: 18g | Fiber: 2g | Carbs: 5g | Protein: 20g	Calories: 492 | Total Fat: 36.2g | Carbs: 34.8g | Protein: 11.1g

Week 4

This is the final stage of our 4 week's keto diet meal plan. In this stage, you already have formed a habit of maintaining a keto diet. So, follow this final stage to get best the best result in your body and mind.

Meal Plan	Breakfast	Snack	Lunch	Dinner	Snack
Day-1	Eggs Ramekins	Spicy Mango Okra (2 servings)	Beef & Potato	Stevia Cod	Broccoli Hash Brown (2 servings)
	Calories: 144 | Fat: 8g | Fiber: 4.5g | Carbs: 9.1g | Protein: 8.8g	Calories: 35 | Total Fat: 0.11g | Carbs: 7.7g | Protein: 2.27g	Calories: 296 | Total Fat: 12.2g | Carbs: 11.8g | Protein: 16.3g	Calories: 267 | Fat: 18g | Fiber: 2g | Carbs: 5g | Protein: 20g	Calories: 93 | Fat: 6.9g | Fiber: 1.3g | Carbs: 3.5g | Protein: 5.5g
Day-2	Greek-Style Frittata with Herbs	Broccoli Hash Brown (2 servings)	Creamy Cheesy Bacon Dip	Cranberry Cod	Paprika Chips (2 servings)
	Calories: 345 | Fat: 28.5g | Carbs: 4.4g | Protein: 18.2g | Fiber: 0.6g	Calories: 93 | Fat: 6.9g | Fiber: 1.3g | Carbs: 3.5g | Protein: 5.5g	Calories: 271 | Fat: 22.5g | Fiber: 0g | Carbs: 1g | Protein: 15.6g	Calories: 289 | Total Fat: 9.2g | Carbs: 8.3g | Protein: 14.3g	Calories: 62 | Total Fat: 6.5g | Carbs: 41.5g | Protein: 5.3g
Day-3	Cheese Mix	Cheese Rounds	Fish Taco	Baked Beef Bowl	Cheese Rounds
	Calories: 209 | Fat: 18.7g | Fiber: 0.9g | Carbs: 2.8g | Protein: 2.9g	Calories: 114 | Fat: 9.4g | Fiber: 0g | Carbs: 0.4g | Protein: 7g	Calories: 302 | Total Fat: 9.2g | Carbs: 8.7g | Protein: 15.2g	Calories: 446 | Fat: 15.5g | Fiber: 1.5g | Carbs: 2.9g | Protein: 69.4g	Calories: 114 | Fat: 9.4g | Fiber: 0g | Carbs: 0.4g | Protein: 7g
Day-4	Breakfast Coconut Porridge	Ham Cheese Egg Cups	Parsnip Fries	Hearty Pork Stew	Spicy Mango Okra
	Calories: 169 | Total Fat: 18.2g | Carbs: 9.3g | Protein: 4.2g	Calories: 137 | Fat: 8.6g | Carbs: 1.8g | Protein: 12g | Fiber: 0.4g	Calories: 262g | Total Fat: 11.3g | Carbs: 10.4g | Protein: 7.2g	Calories: 332 | Fat: 14.7g | Carbs: 3.9g | Protein: 41g | Fiber: 0.8g	Calories: 35 | Total Fat: 0.11g | Carbs: 7.7g | Protein: 2.27g

Day-5	Chili Eggs	Broccoli Hash Brown (2 servings)	Beef & Mushrooms	Saucy Pork Cutlets	Saucy and Spicy Spareribs
	Calories: 64 | Fat: 4.5g | Fiber: 0.1g | Carbs: 0.4g | Protein: 5.6g	Calories: 93 | Fat: 6.9g | Fiber: 1.3g | Carbs: 3.5g | Protein: 5.5g	Calories: 296 | Total Fat: 12.4g | Carbs: 11.3g | Protein: 16.2g	Calories: 369 | Fat: 20.6g | Carbs: 1.1g | Protein: 40.1g | Fiber: 0.1g	Calories: 344 | Fat: 13.6g | Carbs: 4.9g | Protein: 49.5g | Fiber: 1.2g
Day-6	Cheese Muffins (2 servings)	Saucy and Spicy Spareribs	Beef & Mushrooms	Saucy Pork Cutlets	Broccoli Hash Brown (2 servings)
	Calories: 110 | Fat: 7.1g | Fiber: 1.1g | Carbs: 2g | Protein: 9.5g	Calories: 344 | Fat: 13.6g | Carbs: 4.9g | Protein: 49.5g | Fiber: 1.2g	Calories: 296 | Total Fat: 12.4g | Carbs: 11.3g | Protein: 16.2g	Calories: 369 | Fat: 20.6g | Carbs: 1.1g | Protein: 40.1g | Fiber: 0.1g	Calories: 93 | Fat: 6.9g | Fiber: 1.3g | Carbs: 3.5g | Protein: 5.5g
Day-7	Flax Meal Porridge	Parm Bites	Onion Shrimps	Old Bay Crispy Chicken Wings	Parm Bites
	Calories: 298 | Total Fat: 26.7g | Carbs: 13.3 g | Protein: 6.2g	Calories: 136 | Fat: 6.2g | Fiber: 7.7g | Carbs: 13.7g | Protein: 9.4g	Calories: 185 | Fat: 2.8g | Fiber: 0.1g | Carbs: 3g | Protein: 34.5g	Calories: 302 | Total Fat: 11.5g | Carbs: 9.6g | Protein: 16.3g	Calories: 136 | Fat: 6.2g | Fiber: 7.7g | Carbs: 13.7g | Protein: 9.4g

Chapter 3
Breakfast

Breakfast Coconut Porridge

Prep Time: 3 minutes | Cook Time: 7 minutes | Serves 4

- 1 cup coconut milk
- 3 tablespoons blackberries
- 2 tablespoons walnuts
- 1 teaspoon butter
- 1 teaspoon ground cinnamon
- 5 tablespoons chia seeds
- 3 tablespoons coconut flakes
- ¼ teaspoon salt

1. Pour the coconut milk into the air fryer basket tray. Add the coconut, salt, chia seeds, ground cinnamon, and butter. Ground up the walnuts and add them to the air fryer basket tray. Sprinkle the mixture with salt. Mash the blackberries with a fork and add them also to the air fryer basket tray. Cook the porridge at 375°Fahrenheit for 7-minutes.
2. When the cook time is over, remove the air fryer basket from air fryer and allow to sit and rest for 5-minutes. Stir porridge with a wooden spoon and serve warm.

PER SERVING

Calories: 169 | Total Fat: 18.2g | Carbs: 9.3g | Protein: 4.2g

Egg Butter

Prep Time: 5 minutes | Cook Time: 17 minutes | Serves 4

- 4 eggs
- 4 tablespoons butter
- 1 teaspoon salt

1. Cover the air fryer basket with foil and place the eggs there. Transfer the air fryer basket into the air fryer and cook the eggs for 17 minutes at 320°Fahrenheit.
2. When the time is over, remove the eggs from the air fryer basket and put them in cold water to chill them. After this, peel the eggs and chop them up finely. Combine the chopped eggs with butter and add salt. Mix it until you get the spread texture. Serve the egg butter with the keto almond bread.

PER SERVING

Calories: 164 | Total Fat: 8.5g | Carbs: 2.67g | Protein: 3g

Flax Meal Porridge
Prep Time: 5 minutes | Cook Time: 8 minutes | Serves 4

- 2 tablespoons sesame seeds
- ½ teaspoon vanilla extract
- 1 tablespoon butter
- 1 tablespoon liquid Stevia
- 3 tablespoons flax meal
- 1 cup almond milk
- 4 tablespoons chia seeds

1. Preheat your air fryer to 375°Fahrenheit. Put the sesame seeds, chia seeds, almond milk, flax meal, liquid Stevia and butter into the air fryer basket tray. Add the vanilla extract and cook porridge for 8-minutes.
2. When porridge is cooked stir it carefully then allow it to rest for 5-minutes before serving.

PER SERVING
Calories: 298 | Total Fat: 26.7g | Carbs: 13.3 g | Protein: 6.2g

Scrambled Pancake Hash
Prep Time: 3 minutes | Cook Time: 9 minutes | Serves 7

- 1 egg
- ¼ cup heavy cream
- 5 tablespoons butter
- 1 cup coconut flour
- 1 teaspoon ground ginger
- 1 teaspoon salt
- 1 tablespoon apple cider vinegar
- 1 teaspoon baking soda

1. Combine the salt, baking soda, ground ginger and flour in a mixing bowl. In a separate bowl crack, the egg into it. Add butter and heavy cream. Mix well using a hand mixer. Combine the liquid and dry mixtures and stir until smooth.
2. Preheat your air fryer to 400°Fahrenheit. Pour the pancake mixture into the air fryer basket tray. Cook the pancake hash for 4-minutes. After this, scramble the pancake hash well and continue to cook for another 5-minutes more.
3. When dish is cooked, transfer it to serving plates, and serve hot!

PER SERVING
Calories: 178 | Total Fat: 13.3g | Carbs: 10.7g | Protein: 4.4g

Morning Time Sausages

Prep Time: 5 minutes | Cook Time: 12 minutes | Serves 6

- 7-ounces ground chicken
- 7-ounces ground pork
- 1 teaspoon ground coriander
- 1 teaspoon basil, dried
- ½ teaspoon nutmeg
- 1 teaspoon olive oil
- 1 teaspoon minced garlic
- 1 tablespoon coconut flour
- 1 egg
- 1 teaspoon soy sauce
- 1 teaspoon sea salt
- ½ teaspoon ground black pepper

1. Combine the ground pork, chicken, soy sauce, ground black pepper, garlic, basil, coriander, nutmeg, sea salt, and egg. Add the coconut flour and mix the mixture well to combine.
2. Preheat your air fryer to 360°Fahrenheit. Make medium-sized sausages with the ground meat mixture. Spray the inside of the air fryer basket tray with the olive oil. Place prepared sausages into the air fryer basket and place inside of air fryer. Cook the sausages for 6-minutes. Turn the sausages over and cook for 6-minutes more. When the cook time is completed, let the sausages chill for a little bit. Serve warm.

PER SERVING

Calories: 156 | Total Fat: 7.5g | Carbs: 1.3g | Protein: 20.2g

Chicken Muffins

Prep Time: 10 minutes | Cook Time: 10 minutes | Serves 6

- 1 cup ground chicken
- 1 cup ground pork
- ½ cup Mozzarella, shredded
- 1 teaspoon dried oregano
- ½ teaspoon salt
- 1 teaspoon ground paprika
- ½ teaspoon white pepper
- 1 tablespoon ghee, melted
- 1 teaspoon dried dill
- 2 tablespoons almond flour
- 1 egg, beaten

1. In the bowl mix up ground chicken, ground pork, dried oregano, salt, ground paprika, white pepper, dried dill, almond flour, and egg. When you get the homogenous texture of the mass, add ½ of all Mozzarella and mix up the mixture gently with the help of the spoon. Then brush the silicone muffin molds with melted ghee.
2. Put the meat mixture in the muffin molds. Flatten the surface of every muffin with the help of the spoon and top with remaining Mozzarella. Preheat the air fryer to 375F. Then arrange the muffins in the air fryer basket and cook them for 10 minutes. Cool the cooked muffins to the room temperature and remove from the muffin molds.

PER SERVING

Calories: 291 | Fat: 20.6g | Fiber: 1.3g | Carbs: 2.7g | Protein: 23.9g

Spiced Eggs

Prep Time: 10 minutes | Cook Time: 20 minutes | Serves 4

- 8 eggs
- 1 teaspoon dried basil
- 1 teaspoon ground black pepper
- 1 teaspoon dried oregano
- 1 teaspoon avocado oil

1. Brush the air fryer basket with avocado oil from inside.
2. Then crack the eggs inside and top them with ground black pepper and dried oregano.
3. Bake the meal at 355F for 20 minutes.

PER SERVING
Calories: 130 fat 9g | Fiber: 0.4g | Carbs: 1.3g | Protein: 11.2g

Olives and Eggs Mix

Prep Time: 5 minutes | Cook Time: 20 minutes | Serves 4

- 2 cups black olives, pitted and chopped
- 4 eggs, whisked
- ¼ teaspoon sweet paprika
- 1 tablespoon cilantro, chopped
- ½ cup cheddar, shredded
- A pinch of salt and black pepper
- Cooking spray

1. In a bowl, mix the eggs with the olives and all the ingredients except the cooking spray and stir well.
2. Heat up your air fryer at 350 degrees F, grease it with cooking spray, pour the olives and eggs mixture, spread and cook for 20 minutes.
3. Divide between plates and serve for breakfast.

PER SERVING
Calories: 240 | Fat: 14g | Fiber: 3g | Carbs: 5g | Protein: 8g

Cheesy Frittata

Prep Time: 10 minutes | Cook Time: 20 minutes | Serves 6

- 1 cup almond milk
- Cooking spray
- 9 ounces cream cheese, soft
- 1 cup cheddar cheese, shredded
- 6 spring onions, chopped
- Salt and black pepper to the taste
- 6 eggs, whisked

1. Heat up your air fryer with the oil at 350 degrees F and grease it with cooking spray.
2. In a bowl, mix the eggs with the rest of the ingredients, whisk well, pour and spread into the air fryer and cook everything for 20 minutes. Divide everything between plates and serve.

PER SERVING

Calories: 231 | Fat: 11g | Fiber: 3g | Carbs: 5g | Protein: 8g

Herbed Omelet

Prep Time: 5 minutes | Cook Time: 20 minutes | Serves 4

- 10 eggs, whisked
- ½ cup cheddar, shredded
- 2 tablespoons parsley, chopped
- 2 tablespoons chives, chopped
- 2 tablespoons basil, chopped
- Cooking spray
- Salt and black pepper to the taste

1. In a bowl, mix the eggs with all the ingredients except the cheese and the cooking spray and whisk well.
2. Preheat the air fryer at 350 degrees F, grease it with the cooking spray, and pour the eggs mixture inside. Sprinkle the cheese on top and cook for 20 minutes.
3. Divide everything between plates and serve.

PER SERVING

Calories: 232 | Fat: 12g | Fiber: 4g | Carbs: 5g | Protein: 7g

Eggs Ramekins
Prep Time: 5 minutes | Cook Time: 6 minutes | Serves 5

- 5 eggs
- 1 teaspoon coconut oil, melted
- ¼ teaspoon ground black pepper

1. Brush the ramekins with coconut oil and crack the eggs inside. Then sprinkle the eggs with ground black pepper and transfer in the air fryer. Cook the baked eggs for 6 minutes at 355F.

PER SERVING

Calories: 144 | Fat: 8g | Fiber: 4.5g | Carbs: 9.1g | Protein: 8.8g

Paprika Omelet with Goat Cheese
Prep Time: 5 minutes | Cook Time: 10 minutes | Serves 2

- 2 teaspoons ghee, room temperature
- 4 eggs, whisked
- 4 tablespoons goat cheese
- 1 teaspoon paprika
- Sea salt and ground black pepper, to taste

1. Melt the ghee in a pan over medium heat.
2. Add the whisked eggs to the pan and cover with the lid; reduce the heat to medium-low.
3. Cook for 4 minutes; now, stir in the cheese and paprika; continue to cook an additional 3 minutes or until cheese has melted.
4. Season with salt and pepper and serve immediately. Enjoy!

PER SERVING

Calories: 287 | Fat: 22.6g | Carbs: 1.3g | Protein: 19.8g | Fiber: 0g

Cheese Mix

Prep Time: 10 minutes | Cook Time: 20 minutes | Serves 6

- 1 cup of coconut milk
- 1 teaspoon avocado oil
- 2 tablespoons mascarpone
- 1 cup cheddar cheese, shredded
- 3 eggs, beaten

1. Brush the air fryer basket with avocado oil.
2. Then mix coconut milk with mascarpone, cheese, and eggs.
3. Pour the liquid in the air fryer basket and cook it at 350F for 20 minutes.

PER SERVING

Calories: 209 | Fat: 18.7g | Fiber: 0.9g | Carbs: 2.8g | Protein: 2.9g

Chili Eggs

Prep Time: 5 minutes | Cook Time: 6 minutes | Serves 5

- 5 eggs
- 1 teaspoon chili flakes
- 1 teaspoon avocado oil

1. Brush the air fryer basket with avocado oil and crack the eggs inside.
2. Sprinkle the eggs with chili flakes and bake them at 360F for 6 minutes.

PER SERVING

Calories: 64 | Fat: 4.5g | Fiber: 0.1g | Carbs: 0.4g | Protein: 5.6g

Cheese Muffins
Prep Time: 10 minutes | Cook Time: 10 minutes | Serves 6

- 1 cup ground chicken
- ½ cup Cheddar cheese, shredded
- 1 teaspoon dried oregano
- ½ teaspoon salt
- 1 tablespoon butter, softened
- 1 teaspoon dried parsley
- 2 tablespoons coconut flour

1. Mix all ingredients in the mixing bowl and stir until homogenous.
2. Then pour the muffin mixture in the muffin molds and transfer the molds in the air fryer.
3. Bake the muffins at 375F for 10 minutes.

PER SERVING

Calories: 110 | Fat: 7.1g | Fiber: 1.1g | Carbs: 2g | Protein: 9.5g

Dilly Boiled Eggs with Avocado
Prep Time: 5 minutes | Cook Time: 10 minutes | Serves 3

- 6 eggs
- 1/2 teaspoon kosher salt
- 1/2 teaspoon ground black pepper
- 1/2 teaspoon cayenne pepper
- 1/2 teaspoon dried dill weed
- 1 avocado, pitted and sliced
- 1 tablespoon lemon juice

1. Place the eggs in a pan of boiling water; then, cook over low heat for 6 minutes.
2. Peel and halve the eggs. Sprinkle the eggs with salt, black pepper, cayenne pepper, and dill.
3. Serve on individual plates; drizzle the avocado slices with fresh lemon juice and serve with eggs. Enjoy!

PER SERVING

Calories: 222 | Fat: 17.6g | Carbs: 5.7g | Protein: 12.2g | Fiber: 3.9g

Greek-Style Frittata with Herbs
Prep Time: 10 minutes | Cook Time: 30 minutes | Serves 4

- 6 eggs
- 1/2 cup heavy cream
- 2 tablespoons Greek-style yogurt
- 2 ounces bacon, chopped
- Sea salt and freshly ground black pepper, to taste
- 1 tablespoon olive oil
- 1/2 cup red onions, peeled and sliced
- 1 garlic clove, finely chopped
- 8 Kalamata olives, pitted and sliced
- 1 teaspoon dried oregano
- 1/2 teaspoon dried rosemary
- 1/2 teaspoon dried marjoram
- 4 ounces Feta cheese, crumbled

1. Preheat your oven to 360 degrees F. Sprits a baking pan with a nonstick cooking spray.
2. Mix the eggs, cream, yogurt, bacon, salt, and black pepper.
3. Heat the oil in a skillet over medium-high heat. Now, cook the onion and garlic until tender and fragrant, about 3 minutes. Transfer the mixture to the prepared baking pan. Pour the egg mixture over the vegetables. Add olives, oregano, rosemary, and marjoram.
4. Bake approximately 13 minutes, until the eggs are set. Scatter feta cheese over the top and bake an additional 3 minutes. Let it sit for 5 minutes; slice into wedges and serve

PER SERVING

Calories: 345 | Fat: 28.5g | Carbs: 4.4g | Protein: 18.2g | Fiber: 0.6g

Chapter 4
Snacks & Appetizers

Spicy Mango Okra

Prep Time: 5 minutes | Cook Time: 25 minutes | Serves 5

- 35-ounces Okra, washed, drained and wiped dry
- 1 teaspoon red chili powder
- 2 tablespoons coriander powder
- 2 tablespoons almond flour
- 1 ½ tablespoons olive oil
- Pinch of caraway seeds
- Pinch of Fenugreek seeds
- Pinch of Asafoetida
- ½ teaspoon turmeric
- 2 green chilies
- 4 teaspoons dry mango powder
- Salt to taste

1. Slit the okra lengthwise into half. Brush some olive oil on okra then fry in the air fryer. Heat some oil in a pan and add the asafetida, heating it for 10-seconds.
2. Add the fenugreek and caraway seeds, fry them for 10-seconds. Stir in the almond flour and cook for 10-minutes.
3. Mix in the air fried okra and sprinkle the spices on top. Cook for 10-minutes, adding the green chilies cook for an additional 2-minutes.

PER SERVING

Calories: 35 | Total Fat: 0.11g | Carbs: 7.7g | Protein: 2.27g

Parsley & Garlic Flavored Potatoes

Prep Time: 10 minutes | Cook Time: 40 minutes | Serves 4

- 3 Idaho baking potatoes (pricked with a fork)
- 2 tablespoons olive oil
- 1 teaspoon parsley
- 1 tablespoon garlic, minced
- Salt to taste

1. Stir ingredients together in a bowl. Rub the potatoes with the mix. Place them into air fryer basket and cook for 40-minutes at 390°Fahrenheit. Toss twice during cook time.

PER SERVING

Calories: 97 | Total Fat: 0.64g | Carbs: 25.2g | Protein: 10.2g

Turmeric & Garlic Roasted Carrots

Prep Time: 5 minutes | **Cook Time:** 20 minutes | **Serves 4**

- 21-ounces of carrots, peeled
- 1 handful of fresh coriander
- 1 teaspoon turmeric
- 1 tablespoon olive oil
- 1 teaspoon garlic, minced

1. Lightly drizzle the olive oil over the carrots and sprinkle the turmeric and garlic over them. Place in pan in air fryer and cook for 20-minutes at 290°Fahrenheit. Toss once during cook time. Serve carrots garnished with fresh coriander.

PER SERVING

Calories: 60 | Total Fat: 0.35g | Carbs: 10.2g | Protein: 0.48g

Paprika Chips

Prep Time: 10 minutes | **Cook Time:** 40 minutes | **Serves 4**

- 31-ounces of sweet potatoes, peeled and cut into chips
- ½ teaspoon salt
- 2 tablespoons olive oil
- ½ tablespoon paprika

1. Toss all the ingredients together in a bowl. Place in a pan inside your air fryer and cook for 40-minutes at 300°Fahrenheit.

PER SERVING

Calories: 62 | Total Fat: 6.5g | Carbs: 41.5g | Protein: 5.3g

Bacon & Veggie Mash

Prep Time: 15 minutes | Cook Time: 1 hour 15 minutes | Serves 8

- 4 strips of bacon, chopped into pieces
- 1 tablespoon butter
- ¾ cup Yellow onion, diced
- ½ cup red bell pepper, diced
- ¼ cup celery, diced
- 2 teaspoons garlic, minced
- ¾ teaspoon fresh thyme leaves
- 1 ½ cups whole milk
- 3 eggs
- ½ cup heavy cream
- 1 teaspoon sea salt
- ¼ teaspoon cayenne pepper
- 3 cups day-old bread, cubed
- 3 tablespoons parmesan cheese, grated
- 1 cup Monterey Jack cheese grated
- 2 ½ teaspoons paprika
- 2 teaspoons salt
- 2 teaspoons garlic powder
- 1 teaspoon black pepper
- 1 teaspoon onion powder
- 1 teaspoon cayenne pepper
- 1 teaspoon oregano, dried
- 1 teaspoon thyme, dried

1. Grease a casserole dish with the butter. Cook bacon in small frying pan until crisp, then place aside. Cook the corn in the pan until caramelized for about 10-minutes, then add in celery, onion, bell pepper and cook for an additional 5-minutes.
2. Mix in the thyme and garlic and remove from heat. Stir in the eggs, milk, and cream, whisking well to combine. Add in salt, cayenne pepper, bread and Monterey Jack cheese. Transfer to casserole dish and place in air fryer basket. Cook for 30-minutes at 320°Fahrenheit. Sprinkle with parmesan cheese and cook for another 30-minutes.

PER SERVING

Calories: 42 | Total Fat: 8.3g | Carbs: 9.5g | Protein: 16.2g

Coconut Cheese Sticks

Prep Time: 10 minutes | Cook Time: 4 minutes | Serves 4

- 1 egg, beaten
- 4 tablespoons coconut flakes
- 1 teaspoon ground paprika
- 6 oz Provolone cheese
- Cooking spray

1. Cut the cheese into sticks. Then dip every cheese stick in the beaten egg. After this, mix up coconut flakes and ground paprika. Coat the cheese sticks in the coconut mixture.
2. Preheat the air fryer to 400F. Put the cheese sticks in the air fryer and spray them with cooking spray. Cook the meal for 2 minutes from each side. Cool them well before serving.

PER SERVING

Calories: 184 | Fat: 14.2g | Fiber: 0.7g | Carbs: 2.1g | Protein: 12.5g

Sprouts Wraps

Prep Time: 5 minutes | Cook Time: 20 minutes | Serves 12

- 12 bacon strips
- 12 Brussels sprouts
- A drizzle of olive oil

1. Wrap each Brussels sprouts in a bacon strip, brush them with some oil, put them in your air fryer's basket and cook at 350 degrees F for 20 minutes. Serve as an appetizer.

PER SERVING

Calories: 140 | Fat: 5g | Fiber: 2g | Carbs: 4g | Protein: 4g

Broccoli Puree

Prep Time: 10 minutes | Cook Time: 20 minutes | Serves 4

- 1-pound broccoli, chopped
- 1 tablespoon coconut oil
- ¼ cup heavy cream
- 1 teaspoon salt

1. Put coconut oil in the air fryer.
2. Add broccoli, heavy cream, and salt.
3. Cook the mixture for 20 minutes at 365F.
4. Then mash the cooked broccoli mixture until you get the soft puree

PER SERVING

Calories: 94 | Fat: 6.6g | Fiber: 3g | Carbs: 7.7g | Protein: 3.3g

Zucchini Chips

Prep Time: 5 minutes | Cook Time: 15 minutes | Serves 6

- 3 zucchinis, thinly sliced
- Salt and black pepper to the taste
- 2 eggs, whisked
- 1 cup almond flour

1. In a bowl, mix the eggs with salt and pepper. Put the flour in a second bowl. Dredge the zucchinis in flour and then in eggs.
2. Arrange the chips in your air fryer's basket, cook at 350 degrees F for 15 minutes and serve as a snack.

PER SERVING

Calories: 120 | Fat: 4g | Fiber: 2g | Carbs: 3g | Protein: 5g

Chives and Spinach

Prep Time: 5 minutes | Cook Time: 10 minutes | Serves 4

- 3 cups spinach, chopped
- 1 oz chives, chopped
- ½ cup heavy cream
- 1 teaspoon chili powder

1. Mix spinach with chives, heavy cream, and chili powder.
2. Put the mixture in the air fryer basket and cook at 360F for 10 minutes.
3. Carefully mix the meal before serving.

PER SERVING

Calories: 61 | Fat: 5.8g | Fiber: 0.9g | Carbs: 1.9g | Protein: 1.3g

Chili Zucchini Tots

Prep Time: 10 minutes | Cook Time: 12 minutes | Serves 4

- 3 zucchinis, grated
- ½ cup coconut flour
- 2 eggs, beaten
- 1 teaspoon chili flakes
- 1 teaspoon salt
- 1 teaspoon avocado oil

1. In the bowl mix up grated carrot, salt, ground cumin, zucchini, Provolone cheese, chili flakes, egg, and coconut flour. Stir the mass with the help of the spoon and make the small balls. Then line the air fryer basket with baking paper and sprinkle it with sunflower oil.
2. Put the zucchini balls in the air fryer basket and cook them for 12 minutes at 375F. Shake the balls every 2 minutes to avoid burning.

PER SERVING

Calories: 122 | Fat: 7.4g | Fiber: 3.7g | Carbs: 7.3g | Protein: 7.2g

Ham Cheese Egg Cups

Prep Time: 5 minutes | Cook Time: 15 minutes | Serves 9

- 9 slices ham
- Coarse salt and ground black pepper, to season
- 1 teaspoon jalapeno pepper, deseeded and minced
- 1/2 cup Swiss cheese, shredded
- 9 eggs

1. Begin by preheating your oven to 390 degrees F. Lightly grease a muffin pan with cooking spray.
2. Line each cup with a slice of ham; add salt, black pepper, jalapeno, and cheese. Crack an egg into each ham cup.
3. Bake in the preheated oven about 13 minutes or until the eggs are cooked through. Bon appétit!

PER SERVING

Calories: 137 | Fat: 8.6g | Carbs: 1.8g | Protein: 12g | Fiber: 0.4g

Broccoli Hash Brown

Prep Time: 5 minutes | Cook Time: 15 minutes | Serves 4

- 2 cups broccoli, chopped
- 3 eggs, whisked
- 1 tablespoon coconut oil
- 1 teaspoon dried oregano

1. Mix broccoli with eggs and put the mixture in the air fryer.
2. Add coconut oil and dried oregano.
3. Cook the meal at 400F for 15 minutes. Stir the meal every 5 minutes.

PER SERVING

Calories: 93 | Fat: 6.9g | Fiber: 1.3g | Carbs: 3.5g | Protein: 5.5g

Cheese Rounds

Prep Time: 10 minutes | Cook Time: 6 minutes | Serves 4

- 1 cup Cheddar cheese, shredded

1. Preheat the air fryer to 400F. Then line the air fryer basket with baking paper. Sprinkle the cheese on the baking paper in the shape of small rounds. Cook them for 6 minutes or until the cheese is melted and starts to be crispy.

PER SERVING

Calories: 114 | Fat: 9.4g | Fiber: 0g | Carbs: 0.4g | Protein: 7g

Bacon Avocado Wraps

Prep Time: 5 minutes | Cook Time: 15 minutes | Serves 4

- 2 avocados, peeled, pitted and cut into 12 wedges
- 12 bacon strips
- 1 tablespoon ghee, melted

1. Wrap each avocado wedge in a bacon strip, brush them with the ghee, put them in your air fryer's basket and cook at 360 degrees F for 15 minutes. Serve as an appetizer.

PER SERVING

Calories: 161 | Fat: 4g | Fiber: 2g | Carbs: 4g | Protein: 6g

Saucy and Spicy Spareribs

Prep Time: 10 minutes | Cook Time: 2 hours 35 minutes | Serves 4

- 2 pounds St. Louis-style spareribs
- 1 tablespoon Fajita seasoning mix
- 2 cloves garlic, pressed
- 1/2 cup chicken bone broth
- 1 cup tomato sauce

1. Toss the spareribs with the Fajita seasoning mix, garlic, chicken bone broth, and tomato sauce until well coated.
2. Arrange the spare ribs on a tinfoil-lined baking sheet.
3. Bake in the preheated oven at 260 degrees F for 2 hours and 30 minutes.
4. Place under the preheated broiler for about 8 minutes until the sauce is lightly caramelized. Bon appétit!

PER SERVING

Calories: 344 | Fat: 13.6g | Carbs: 4.9g | Protein: 49.5g | Fiber: 1.2g

Parm Bites

Prep Time: 10 minutes | Cook Time: 10 minutes | Serves 5

- 2 medium eggplants, trimmed, sliced
- 4 oz Parmesan, grated
- 1 teaspoon coconut oil, melted

1. Grease the air fryer basket with coconut oil.
2. Then put the sliced eggplants in the air fryer basket in one layer.
3. Top them with Parmesan and cook the meal at 390F for 10 minutes

PER SERVING

Calories: 136 | Fat: 6.2g | Fiber: 7.7g | Carbs: 13.7g | Protein: 9.4g

Taco Chicken Wings

Prep Time: 15 minutes | Cook Time: 1 hour | Serves 5

- 2 tablespoons extra-virgin olive oil
- 2 pounds chicken wings
- 1 tablespoon whiskey
- 1 tablespoon Taco seasoning mix
- 1 cup tomato sauce

1. Start by preheating your oven to 410 degrees F. Toss the chicken wings with the other ingredients until well coated.
2. Place the wings onto a rack in the baking pan. Bake in the preheated oven for 50 to 55 minutes until a meat thermometer reads 165 degrees F.
3. Serve with dipping sauce, if desired. Enjoy!

PER SERVING

Calories: 293 | Fat: 12.1g | Carbs: 3.4g | Protein: 40.6g | Fiber: 0.9g

Ham and Avocado Stuffed Eggs

Prep Time: 5 minutes | **Cook Time:** 20 minutes | **Serves 4**

- 4 large eggs
- 1/2 avocado, mashed
- 1/2 teaspoon yellow mustard
- 1 garlic clove, minced
- 2 ounces cooked ham, chopped

1. Place the eggs in a saucepan and fill with enough water. Bring the water to a rolling boil; heat off. Cover and allow the eggs to sit for about 12 minutes; let them cool.
2. Slice the eggs into halves; mix the yolks with the avocado, mustard and garlic.
3. Dive the avocado filling among the egg whites. Top with the chopped ham. Bon appétit!

PER SERVING

Calories: 128 | Fat: 8.9g | Carbs: 2.9g | Protein: 9.2g | Fiber: 1.7g

Two Cheese and Prosciutto Balls

Prep Time: 5 minutes | **Cook Time:** 10 minutes | **Serves 4**

- 2 ounces goat cheese, crumbled
- 2 ounces feta cheese crumbled
- 3 ounces prosciutto, chopped
- 1 red bell pepper, deveined and finely chopped
- 2 tablespoons sesame seeds, toasted

1. Thoroughly combine the cheese, prosciutto and pepper until everything is well incorporated. Shape the mixture into balls.
2. Arrange these keto balls on a platter and place them in the refrigerator until ready to serve.
3. Roll the keto balls in toasted sesame seeds before serving. Bon appétit!

PER SERVING

Calories: 176 | Fat: 12.9g | Carbs: 2.3g | Protein: 12.8g | Fiber: 0.6g

Stuffed Mini Peppers

Prep Time: 5 minutes | **Cook Time:** 25 minutes | **Serves 6**

- 3/4 pound ground beef
- 1/2 cup onion, chopped
- 2 garlic cloves, minced
- 12 mini peppers, deveined
- 1/2 cup cheddar cheese, shredded

1. Heat up a lightly oiled sauté pan over a moderate flame. Brown the ground beef for 3 to 4 minutes, crumbling with a fork.
2. Stir in the onions and garlic; continue to sauté an additional 2 minutes or until tender and aromatic.
3. Cook the peppers in boiling water until just tender or approximately 7 minutes.
4. Arrange the stuffed peppers on a tinfoil-lined baking pan. Divide the beef mixture among the peppers. Top with the shredded cheddar cheese.
5. Bake in the preheated oven at 360 degrees F approximately 17 minutes. Serve at room temperature. Bon appétit!

PER SERVING

Calories: 207 | Fat: 10.2g | Carbs: 6.8g | Protein: 19.7g | Fiber: 1.6g

Chapter 5
Chicken and Poultry

Chicken with Sauce, Vegetables & Rice
Prep Time: 5 minutes | **Cook Time:** 16 minutes | **Serves 4**

- 1 lb. chicken breasts, skinless and boneless
- ½ lb. button mushrooms, sliced
- 1 medium-sized onion, chopped
- 2 cups cooked rice
- 1 jar (10-ounces) Alfredo sauce
- Salt and pepper to taste
- ½ teaspoon thyme, dried

1. Cut the chicken breasts into 1-inch cubes. Mix chicken, onion, and mushrooms in a large bowl. Season with salt and dried thyme and mix well.
2. Preheat your air fryer to 370°Fahrenheit and sprinkle basket with olive oil. Transfer chicken and vegetables to fryer and cook for 12-minutes and stir occasionally. Stir in the Alfredo sauce. Cook for another 4-minutes. Serve with cooked rice.

PER SERVING

Calories: 289 | Total Fat: 11.2g | Carbs: 8.4g | Protein: 15.3g

Philly Chicken Cheesesteak Stromboli
Prep Time: 10 minutes | **Cook Time:** 28 minutes | **Serves 2**

- 2 chicken breasts, boneless,
- skinless, partially frozen
- ½ onion, sliced
- 1 tablespoon Worcestershire sauce
- Sea salt and black pepper to taste
- 14-ounce package of pizza dough
- 1 tablespoon almond flour
- ½ cup jarred cheese sauce, warm
- 1 ½ cup cheddar cheese, grated

1. Thinly slice the chicken breasts. Preheat your air fryer to 400°Fahrenheit. Spray with cooking spray. Add onions and cook for 8-minutes and stir halfway through cook time.
2. Prepare surface for making pizza dough by sprinkling flour. Roll the dough out into 11" x 13" rectangle, with the long side closest to you. Add cheese but leave an empty 1-inch border from edge farthest away from you.
3. Layer the chicken and onion mixture, cover with cheese sauce and sprinkle remaining cheese. Roll Stromboli away from you toward empty border. The filling should stay tightly tucked inside roll. Tuck ends of pizza dough, and pinch seam. Shape the Stromboli into a U-shape, seam side down. Make 4 small slits on top of pizza dough. Brush the Stromboli with oil. Preheat air fryer to 370°Fahrenheit. Grease basket with oil and add Stromboli. Cook for 6-minutes on each side. Set aside and allow to cool for about 3-minutes before serving.

PER SERVING

Calories: 285 | Total Fat: 10.5g | Carbs: 9.2g | Protein: 15.3g

Prawn Paste Chicken Wings
Prep Time: 5 minutes | **Cook Time:** 16 minutes | **Serves 2**

- 1 tablespoon prawn/shrimp paste
- 2 tablespoons olive oil
- 1 teaspoon liquid Stevia
- 1 teaspoon sesame oil
- ½ teaspoon dried ginger
- 2/3 lb. chicken wings

1. In a large bowl, combine all the ingredients, except for the chicken wings. Stir well, then place the chicken on top. Leave for at least an hour.
2. Preheat your air fryer to 350°Fahrenheit. Remove the wings from the marinade, lightly brush them with oil and place into your air fryer. Cook wings for 8-minutes at 350°Fahrenheit.
3. Pull out the tray and using a pair of tongs flip over the wings and place tray back into air fryer for another 8-minutes. Drain the cooked chicken wings on paper towels before serving.

PER SERVING

Calories: 287 | Total Fat: 10.2g | Carbs: 8.6g | Protein: 15.4g

Old Bay Crispy Chicken Wings
Prep Time: 10 minutes | **Cook Time:** 40 minutes | **Serves 4**

- 3 lbs. bone-in chicken wings
- ¾ cup almond flour
- 1 tablespoon Old Bay seasoning
- 2 fresh lemons, juiced
- 4 tablespoons butter

1. In a bowl, mix the Old Bay seasoning and flour. Add chicken wings and toss well to combine.
2. Preheat your air fryer to 375°Fahrenheit. Take off excess flour and transfer the chicken wings into air fryer. Work in batches does not overcrowd. Cook for 40-minutes and often shake while cooking.
3. Melt butter in a sauté pan over low heat. Squeeze the lemon juice from the two lemons into melted butter and to blend. Serve hot wings and pour the lemon butter over them. Serve hot!

PER SERVING

Calories: 302 | Total Fat: 11.5g | Carbs: 9.6g | Protein: 16.3g

Jerk-Style Chicken Wings
Prep Time: 5 minutes | Cook Time: 20 minutes | Serves 5

- 3 lbs. chicken wings
- 2 tablespoons olive oil
- 1 tablespoon fresh thyme, finely chopped
- 1 teaspoon liquid Stevia
- Pinch of white pepper
- Pinch of cayenne pepper
- Pinch of allspice
- 1 habanero pepper, deseeded and chopped
- 6 cloves garlic, finely chopped
- 2 tablespoons soy sauce
- 1 tablespoons fresh ginger, finely grated
- 4 scallions, chopped
- 5 tablespoons lime juice
- ½ cup red wine vinegar
- Salt to taste

1. Prepare the marinade in a bowl, mix all the ingredients, excluding the chicken. Season with salt. Mix marinade and chicken wings in a zip-lock bag, seal the bag and shake to mix contents. Marinate in the fridge for 2-hours.
2. Preheat your air fryer to 350°Fahrenheit. Drain the marinated chicken wings on a paper towel-lined baking sheet and pat dry with more paper towels. Place the chicken inside of air fryer and cook for 10-minutes. Flip over chicken wings and cook for an additional 10-minutes

PER SERVING

Calories: 289 | Total Fat: 11.7g | Carbs: 8.4g | Protein: 14.3g

Parmesan and Dill Chicken
Prep Time: 15 minutes | Cook Time: 20 minutes | Serves 6

- 18 oz chicken breast, skinless, boneless
- 5 oz pork rinds
- 3 oz Parmesan, grated
- 3 eggs, beaten
- 1 teaspoon chili flakes
- 1 teaspoon ground paprika
- 2 tablespoons avocado oil
- 1 teaspoon Erythritol
- ¼ teaspoon onion powder
- 1 teaspoon cayenne pepper
- 1 chili pepper, minced
- ½ teaspoon dried dill

1. In the shallow bowl mix up chili flakes, ground paprika, Erythritol. Onion powder, and cayenne pepper. Add dried dill and stir the mixture gently. Then rub the chicken breast in the spice mixture. Then rub the chicken with minced chili pepper. Dip the chicken breast in the beaten eggs. After this, coat it in the Parmesan and dip in the eggs again. Then coat the chicken in the pork rinds and sprinkle with avocado oil.

2. Preheat the air fryer to 380F. Put the chicken breast in the air fryer and cook it for 16 minutes. Then flip the chicken breast on another side and cook it for 4 minutes more.

PER SERVING

Calories: 318 | Fat: 16.5g | Fiber: 0.5g | Carbs: 1.5g | Protein: 40.7g

Ginger and Coconut Chicken
Prep Time: 5 minutes | Cook Time: 20 minutes | Serves 4

- 4 chicken breasts, skinless, boneless and halved
- 4 tablespoons coconut aminos
- 1 teaspoon olive oil
- 2 tablespoons stevia
- Salt and black pepper to the taste
- ¼ cup chicken stock
- 1 tablespoon ginger, grated

1. In a pan that fits the air fryer, combine the chicken with the ginger and all the ingredients and toss..
2. Put the pan in your air fryer and cook at 4380 degrees F for 20, shaking the fryer halfway. Divide between plates and serve with a side salad.

PER SERVING

Calories: 256 | Fat: 12g | Fiber: 4g | Carbs: 6g | Protein: 14g

Tomato Chicken Mix
Prep Time: 10 minutes | Cook Time: 18 minutes | Serves 4

- pound chicken breast, skinless, boneless
- 1 tablespoon keto tomato sauce
- 1 teaspoon avocado oil
- ½ teaspoon garlic powder

1. In the small bowl mix up tomato sauce, avocado oil, and garlic powder. Then brush the chicken breast with the tomato sauce mixture well.
2. Preheat the air fryer to 385F. Place the chicken breast in the air fryer and cook it for 15 minutes. Then flip it on another side and cook for 3 minutes more. Slice the cooked chicken breast into servings.

PER SERVING

Calories: 139 | Fat: 3g | Fiber: 0.2g | Carbs: 2g | Protein: 24.2 g

Spinach Chicken Wings
Prep Time: 10 minutes | **Cook Time:** 25 minutes | **Serves 4**

- 1 cup fresh spinach, chopped
- 2 tablespoons olive oil
- 1 oz Parmesan, grated
- 1-pound chicken wings, skinless, boneless, chopped

1. Brush the air fryer basket with olive oil from inside.
2. Then put the chicken wings inside.
3. Top them with chopped spinach and Parmesan.
4. Cook the meal at 380F for 25 minutes.

PER SERVING

Calories: 214 | Fat: 11.4g | Fiber: 0.2g | Carbs: 0.5g | Protein: 26.5g

---

Asparagus Chicken
Prep Time: 15 minutes | **Cook Time:** 25 minutes | **Serves 4**

- 1 cup asparagus, chopped
- 1-pound chicken thighs, skinless, boneless
- 1 teaspoon onion powder
- 1 oz scallions, chopped
- 1 tablespoon coconut oil, melted
- 1 teaspoon smoked paprika

1. Mix chicken thighs with onion powder, coconut oil and smoked paprika.
2. Then flip the chicken thighs on another side and top with chopped asparagus and scallions.
3. Cook the meal for 5 minutes more.

PER SERVING

Calories: 257 | Fat: 11.9g | Fiber: 1.1g | Carbs: 2.6g | Protein: 33.8g

---

Buttery Chicken Wings
Prep Time: 5 minutes | **Cook Time:** 30 minutes | **Serves 4**

- 2 pounds chicken wings
- Salt and black pepper to the taste
- 3 garlic cloves, minced
- 3 tablespoons butter, melted
- ½ cup heavy cream
- ½ teaspoon basil, dried
- ½ teaspoon oregano, dried
- ¼ cup parmesan, grated

1. In a baking dish that fits your air fryer, mix the chicken wings with all the ingredients except the parmesan and toss.
2. Put the dish to your air fryer and cook at 380 degrees F for 30 minutes. Sprinkle the cheese on top, leave the mix aside for 10 minutes, divide between plates and serve.

PER SERVING

Calories: 270 | Fat: 12g | Fiber: 3g | Carbs: 6g | Protein: 17g

---

Cream Cheese Chicken Mix
Prep Time: 15 minutes | **Cook Time:** 16 minutes | **Serves 4**

- pound chicken wings
- ¼ cup cream cheese
- 1 tablespoon apple cider vinegar
- 1 teaspoon Truvia
- ½ teaspoon smoked paprika
- 1 teaspoon avocado oil

1. In the mixing bowl mix up cream cheese, Truvia, apple cider vinegar, smoked paprika, and ground nutmeg. Then add the chicken wings and coat them in the cream cheese mixture well.
2. Leave the chicken winds in the cream cheese mixture for 10-15 minutes to marinate. Meanwhile, preheat the air fryer to 380F.
3. Put the chicken wings in the air fryer and cook them for 8 minutes. Then flip the chicken wings on another and brush with cream cheese marinade. Cook the chicken wings for 8 minutes more.

PER SERVING

Calories: 271 | Fat: 13.7g | Fiber: 0.2g | Carbs: 1.2g | Protein: 34g

---

Nutmeg Chicken Fillets
Prep Time: 15 minutes | **Cook Time:** 12 minutes | **Serves 4**

- 16 oz chicken fillets
- 1 teaspoon ground nutmeg
- 1 tablespoon avocado oil
- ½ teaspoon salt

1. Mix ground nutmeg with avocado oil and salt.
2. Then rub the chicken fillet with a nutmeg mixture and put it in the air fryer basket.
3. Cook the meal at 385F for 12 minutes.

PER SERVING

Calories: 223 | Fat: 9g | Fiber: 0.3g | Carbs: 0.5g | Protein: 32.9g

---

Taco Chicken
Prep Time: 15 minutes | **Cook Time:** 30 minutes | **Serves 4**

- 1 tablespoon taco seasonings
- 1 tablespoon apple cider vinegar
- 1 tablespoon olive oil
- 2-pounds chicken thighs, skinless, boneless

1. Rub the chicken thighs with taco seasonings and sprinkle with olive oil and apple cider vinegar.
2. Put them in the air fryer and cook at 365F for 15 minutes per side.

PER SERVING

Calories: 469 | Fat: 20.3g | Fiber: 0g | Carbs: 1.5g | Protein: 65.6g

Chicken Thighs with Kalamata Olives
Prep Time: 10 minutes | Cook Time: 30 minutes | Serves 4

- 8 chicken thighs, boneless, skinless
- 1 tablespoon coconut oil, melted
- 1 teaspoon dried basil
- ½ teaspoon cumin seeds
- 4 kalamata olives, sliced

1. Rub the chicken thighs with coconut oil, dried basil, and cumin seeds.
2. Put the chicken in the air fryer basket and cook t 375F for 20 minutes.
3. Then flip the chicken thighs on another side, top them with Kalamata olives and cook the meals for 10 minutes more.

PER SERVING

Calories: 590 | Fat: 25.6g | Fiber: 0.2g | Carbs: 0.4g | Protein: 84.6g

Sunday Chicken Bake
Prep Time: 10 minutes | Cook Time: 30 minutes | Serves 4

- 1 tablespoon olive oil
- 3/4 pound chicken breast fillets, chopped into bite-sized chunks
- 2 garlic cloves, sliced
- 1/4 teaspoon Korean chili pepper flakes
- 1/4 teaspoon Himalayan salt
- 1/2 teaspoon poultry seasoning mix
- 1 bell pepper, deveined and chopped
- 2 ripe tomatoes, chopped
- 1/4 cup heavy whipping cream
- 1/4 cup sour cream

1. Brush a casserole dish with olive oil. Add the chicken, garlic, Korean chili pepper flakes, salt, and poultry seasoning mix to the casserole dish.
2. Next, layer the pepper and tomatoes. Whisk the heavy whipping cream and sour cream in a mixing bowl.
3. Top everything with the cream mixture. Bake in the preheated oven at 390 degrees F for about 25 minutes or until thoroughly heated. Bon appétit!

PER SERVING

Calories: 410 | Fat: 20.7g | Carbs: 6.2g | Total Carbs: 50g | Fiber: 1.5g

Primavera Stuffed Turkey Fillets
Prep Time: 10 minutes | Cook Time: 1 hour | Serves 6

- 2 tablespoons extra-virgin olive oil
- 1 tablespoon Italian seasoning mix
- Sea salt and freshly ground black pepper, to season
- 2 garlic cloves, sliced
- 6 ounces Asiago cheese, sliced
- 2 bell peppers, thinly sliced
- 1 ½ pounds turkey breasts
- 2 tablespoons Italian parsley, roughly chopped

1. Brush the sides and bottom of a casserole dish with 1 tablespoon of extra-virgin olive oil. Preheat an oven to 360 degrees F.
2. Sprinkle the turkey breast with the Italian seasoning mix, salt, and black pepper on all sides.
3. Make slits in each turkey breast and stuff with garlic, cheese, and bell peppers. Drizzle the turkey breasts with the remaining tablespoon of olive oil.
4. Bake in the preheated oven for 50 minutes or until an instant-read thermometer registers 165 degrees
5. Garnish with Italian parsley and serve warm. Bon appétit!

PER SERVING

Calories: 347 | Fat: 22.2g | Carbs: 3g | Protein: 32g | Fiber: 0.5g

Teriyaki Turkey Bowls
Prep Time: 5 minutes | Cook Time: 15 minutes | Serves 4

- 3/4 pound lean ground turkey
- 1 brown onion, chopped
- 1 red bell pepper, deveined and chopped
- 1 serrano pepper, deveined and chopped
- 1 tablespoon rice vinegar
- 1 garlic clove, pressed
- 1 tablespoon sesame oil
- 1/2 teaspoon ground cumin
- 1/2 teaspoon hot sauce
- 2 tablespoons peanut butter
- Sea salt and cayenne pepper, to season
- 1/2 teaspoon celery seeds
- 1/2 teaspoon mustard seeds
- 1 rosemary sprig, leaves chopped
- 2 tablespoons fresh Thai basil, snipped

1. Heat a medium-sized pan over medium-high heat; once hot, brown the ground turkey for 4 to 6 minutes; reserve.
2. Then cook the onion and peppers in the pan drippings for a further 2 to 3 minutes.
3. Add 1/4 cup of cold water to another saucepan and heat over medium heat. Now, stir in vinegar, garlic, sesame oil, cumin, hot sauce, peanut butter, salt, cayenne pepper, celery seeds, and mustard seeds.
4. Let it simmer, stirring occasionally, until the mixture begins to bubble slightly. Bring the mixture to a boil; then, immediately remove from the heat and add the cooked ground turkey and sautéed onion/pepper mixture.
5. Ladle into serving bowls and garnish with the rosemary and Thai basil. Enjoy!

PER SERVING

Calories: 410 | Fat: 27.1g | Carbs: 6.6g | Total Carbs: 36.5g | Fiber: 1g

Keto TSO Chicken

Prep Time: 25 minutes | **Cook Time:** 22 minutes | **Serves 4**

- pound chicken breast, skinless, boneless, chopped
- 1 tablespoon avocado oil
- 1 teaspoon ground black pepper
- 1 teaspoon salt
- 1 tablespoon coconut aminos
- ½ cup almond flour
- 1 teaspoon Erythritol
- 1 chili pepper, chopped
- 2 oz scallions, chopped
- 1 teaspoon coconut oil
- ¼ cup of water

1. Rub the chicken with avocado oil, ground black pepper, salt, and coconut aminos/
2. Add water and leave the chicken for 15 minutes to marinate.
3. Meanwhile, mix almond flour with Erythritol, chili pepper, and scallions.
4. Coat the chicken in the almond flour mixture and put it in the air fryer. Add coconut oil.
5. Cook the meal at 375F for 11 minutes per side.

PER SERVING

Calories: 238 | Fat: 11.1g | Fiber: 2.2g | Carbs: 6.7g | Protein: 27.4g

---

Chicken with Asparagus and Zucchini

Prep Time: 15 minutes | **Cook Time:** 25 minutes | **Serves 4**

- 1 pound chicken thighs, boneless and skinless
- Juice of 1 lemon
- 2 tablespoons olive oil
- 3 garlic cloves, minced
- 1 teaspoon oregano, dried
- ½ pound asparagus, trimmed and halved
- A pinch of salt and black pepper
- 1 zucchinis, halved lengthwise and sliced into half-moons

1. In a bowl, mix the chicken with all the ingredients except the asparagus and the zucchinis, toss and leave aside for 15 minutes.
2. Add the zucchinis and the asparagus, toss, put everything into a pan that fits the air fryer, and cook at 380 degrees F for 25 minutes. Divide everything between plates and serve.

PER SERVING

Calories: 280 | Fat: 11g | Fiber: 4g | Carbs: 6g | Protein: 17g

---

Greek-Style Chicken Mélange

Prep Time: 10 minutes | **Cook Time:** 35 minutes | **Serves 4**

- 2 ounces bacon, diced
- 3/4 pound whole chicken, boneless and chopped
- 1/2 medium-sized leek, chopped
- 1 teaspoon ginger garlic paste
- 1 teaspoon poultry seasoning mix
- Sea salt, to taste
- 1 bay leaf
- 1 thyme sprig
- 1 rosemary sprig
- 1 cup chicken broth
- 1/2 cup cauliflower, chopped into small florets
- 2 vine-ripe tomatoes, pureed

1. Heat a medium-sized pan over medium-high heat; once hot, fry the bacon until it is crisp or about 3 minutes. Add in the chicken and cook until it is no longer pink; reserve.
2. Pour in the chicken broth and reduce the heat to medium; let it cook for 15 minutes, stirring periodically.
3. Add in the cauliflower and tomatoes along with the reserved bacon and chicken. Decrease the temperature to simmer and let it cook for a further 15 minutes or until warmed through. Bon appétit!

PER SERVING

Calories: 352 | Fat: 14.3g | Carbs: 5.9g | Total Carbs: 44.2g | Fiber: 2.4g

---

Mediterranean Roasted Chicken with Aromatics

Prep Time: 5 minutes | **Cook Time:** 25 minutes | **Serves 5**

- 2 tablespoons olive oil
- 1 ½ pounds chicken drumettes
- 2 cloves garlic, minced
- 1 thyme sprig
- 1 rosemary sprig
- 1/2 teaspoon dried oregano
- 2 tablespoons Greek cooking wine
- 1/2 cup chicken bone broth
- 1 red onion, cut into wedges
- 2 bell peppers, sliced

1. Start by preheating your oven to 420 degrees F. Brush the sides and bottom a baking dish with 1 tablespoon of olive oil.
2. Heat the remaining tablespoon of olive oil in a saucepan over a moderate flame. Brown the chicken drumettes for 5 to 6 minutes per side.
3. Transfer the warm chicken drumettes to a baking dish. Add the garlic, spices, wine and broth. Scatter red onion and peppers around chicken drumettes.
4. Roast in the preheated oven for about 13 minutes. Serve immediately and enjoy!

PER SERVING

Calories: 218 | Fat: 9.1g | Carbs: 4.2g | Protein: 28.6g | Fiber: 0.7g

Chapter 6
Beef, Lamb and Pork

Sausage Balls

Prep Time: 5 minutes | Cook Time: 8 minutes | Serves 5

- 8-ounces ground chicken
- 1 egg white
- 1 teaspoon paprika
- 1 tablespoon olive oil
- 2 tablespoons almond flour
- ½ teaspoon ground black pepper
- ½ teaspoon salt
- 1 tablespoon parsley, dried

1. Whisk the egg white and combine it with the ground chicken in a mixing bowl. Add parsley and salt to the mixture. Add paprika and ground black pepper to mixture and stir. With wet hands make small sausage balls from the ground chicken mixture. Sprinkle each sausage ball with almond flour.
2. Preheat your air fryer to 380°Fahrenheit. Spray the inside of the air fryer basket tray with olive oil. Place the sausage balls into the basket and cook for 8-minutes. Turn the balls to brown all sides during the cooking process. Transfer the cooked sausage balls into serving plates. Serve warm.

PER SERVING

Calories: 180 | Total Fat: 11.8g | Carbs: 2.9g | Protein: 16.3g

Keto Breakfast Bacon

Prep Time: 5 minutes | Cook Time: 10minutes | Serves 4

- 8-ounces bacon, sliced
- ½ teaspoon oregano, dried
- 4-ounces cheddar cheese, shredded
- ½ teaspoon ground black pepper
- ½ teaspoon salt
- ½ teaspoon ground thyme

1. Slice the bacon and rub it with the dried oregano, ground black pepper, salt and ground thyme on each side. Leave the bacon for 3-minutes to soak in the spices.
2. Meanwhile, preheat your air fryer to 360°Fahrenheit. Place the sliced bacon in the air fryer rack and cook for 5-minutes. Meanwhile, shred the cheddar cheese. When the bacon is cooked—sprinkle it with the shredded cheddar cheese and cook for 30-seconds more. Transfer to serving plates and serve warm.

PER SERVING

Calories: 423 | Total Fat: 33.1g | Carbs: 1.5g | Protein: 28.1g

Pork Breakfast Sticks

Prep Time: 5 minutes | Cook Time: 10 minutes | Serves 4

- 10-ounce pork fillet
- 1 tablespoon olive oil
- ½ teaspoon salt
- 1 teaspoon paprika
- 1 teaspoon apple cider vinegar
- 1 teaspoon oregano
- 1 teaspoon nutmeg
- ¼ teaspoon ground ginger
- 1 teaspoon basil, dried
- 5-ounces Parmesan cheese, shredded

1. Cut the pork fillet into thick strips. Combine the nutmeg, ginger, oregano, paprika, and salt in a shallow bowl and stir. Sprinkle the pork strips with the spice mixture. Sprinkle the pork strips with apple cider vinegar.
2. Preheat your air fryer to 380°Fahrenheit. Sprinkle the inside of the air fryer basket with olive oil and place the pork strips inside of it. Cook pork strips for 5-minutes, then turn strips over and cook for 4-minutes more. Cover the pork strips with parmesan cheese and cook for 1-minute more. Remove the pork strips from air fryer and serve immediately

PER SERVING

Calories: 315 | Total Fat: 20.4g | Carbs: 2.2g | Protein: 31.3g

Pork and Garlic Sauce

Prep Time: 5 minutes | Cook Time: 25 minutes | Serves 4

- 1 pound pork tenderloin, sliced
- A pinch of salt and black pepper
- 4 tablespoons butter, melted
- 2 teaspoons garlic, minced
- 1 teaspoon sweet paprika

1. Heat up a pan that fits the air fryer with the butter over medium heat, add all the ingredients except the pork medallions, whisk well and simmer for 4-5 minutes.
2. Add the pork, toss, put the pan in your air fryer and cook at 380 degrees F for 20 minutes. Divide between plates and serve with a side salad.

PER SERVING

Calories: 284 | Fat: 12g | Fiber: 4g | Carbs: 6g | Protein: 19g

Creamy Cheesy Bacon Dip
Prep Time: 15 minutes | Cook Time: 12 minutes | Serves 6

- 6 teaspoon cream cheese
- ½ cup heavy cream
- 1 teaspoon dried sage
- 1 cup Monterey Jack cheese, shredded
- ½ teaspoon chili flakes
- 1 tablespoon chives, chopped
- 1 teaspoon avocado oil
- ½ teaspoon salt
- 6 oz bacon, chopped

1. Preheat the air fryer to 400F. Put the chopped bacon in the air fryer and cook it for 6 minutes. Stir it after 3 minutes of cooking.
2. After this, transfer the cooked bacon in the baking pan. Add cream cheese, heavy cream, Monterey Jack cheese, chili flakes, chives, avocado oil, sage, and salt. Mix up the mixture.
3. Clean the air fryer basket and insert the baking pan with bacon dip inside. Cook it at 385F for 6 minutes.

PER SERVING

Calories: 271 | Fat: 22.5g | Fiber: 0g | Carbs: 1g | Protein: 15.6g

Chili Pork
Prep Time: 5 minutes | Cook Time: 25 minutes | Serves 4

- 2 teaspoons chili paste
- 2 garlic cloves, minced
- 4 pork chops
- 1 shallot, chopped
- 1 and ½ cups coconut milk
- 2 tablespoons olive oil
- 3 tablespoons coconut aminos
- Salt and black pepper to the taste

1. In a pan that fits your air fryer, mix the pork the rest of the ingredients, toss, introduce the pan in the fryer and cook at 400 degrees F for 25 minutes, shaking the fryer halfway.
2. Divide everything into bowls and serve.

PER SERVING

Calories: 267 | Fat: 12g | Fiber: 4g | Carbs: 6g | Protein: 18g

Cilantro Beef Meatballs
Prep Time: 20 minutes | Cook Time: 7 minutes | Serves 4

- 1 cup ground beef
- 3 oz Cheddar cheese, shredded
- 1 tablespoons flax meal
- 1 teaspoon fresh cilantro, chopped
- 1 garlic clove, diced
- 1 chili pepper, chopped
- 1 egg, beaten
- 1 teaspoon ground coriander
- ¼ cup scallions, diced
- ½ teaspoon ground black pepper
- 1 teaspoon avocado oil

1. Put the ground beef in the bowl and mix it up with flax meal, cilantro, garlic clove, chili pepper, egg, ground coriander, diced onion, and ground black pepper. When the mixture is homogenous, add shredded Cheddar cheese and stir the mixture with the help of the spoon.
2. Make the small meatballs from the ground beef mixture. Then preheat the air fryer to 380F. Brush the air fryer basket with avocado oil from inside and arrange the prepared meatballs in one layer. Cook them for 7 minutes or until the meatballs are light brown.

PER SERVING

Calories: 180 | Fat: 13g | Fiber: 0.8g | Carbs: 2.1g | Protein: 13.8g

Beef Under Cabbage Blanket
Prep Time: 10 minutes | Cook Time: 50 minutes | Serves 4

- 2-pounds beef sirloin, diced
- 1 cup white cabbage, shredded
- ½ cup beef broth
- 1 teaspoon taco seasonings
- 1 teaspoon coconut oil
- 1 teaspoon salt

1. Mix beef sirloin with taco seasonings and salt.
2. Put the coconut oil in the air fryer basket. Add beef sirloin and beef broth.
3. Then top the beef with white cabbage.
4. Cook the meal at 360F for 50 minutes.

PER SERVING

Calories: 440 | Fat: 15.5g | Fiber: 0.4g | Carbs: 1.1g | Protein: 69.6g

Basil Pork

Prep Time: 5 minutes | Cook Time: 25 minutes | Serves 4

- 4 pork chops
- A pinch of salt and black pepper
- 2 teaspoons basil, dried
- 2 tablespoons olive oil
- ½ teaspoon chili powder

1. In a pan that fits your air fryer, mix all the ingredients, toss, introduce in the fryer and cook at 400 degrees F for 25 minutes.
2. Divide everything between plates and serve.

PER SERVING

Calories: 274 | Fat: 13g | Fiber: 4g | Carbs: 6g | Protein: 18g

Coconut Beef Steak

Prep Time: 10 minutes | Cook Time: 16 minutes | Serves 4

- 2-pounds beef steak
- 3 tablespoons coconut oil
- 1 teaspoon coconut shred
- 1 teaspoon dried basil

1. Rub the beef steak with coconut shred and dried basil.
2. Then brush the beef steak with coconut oil and put it in the air fryer.
3. Cook the beef steak at 390F for 8 minutes per side.

PER SERVING

Calories: 509 | Fat: 24.3g | Fiber: 0g | Carbs: 0g | Protein: 68.8g

Beef & Potato

Prep Time: 5 minutes | Cook Time: 20 minutes | Serves 4

- 2 eggs
- 3 cups mashed potatoes
- 1 lb. ground beef
- 2 tablespoons garlic powder
- 1 cup sour cream
- Pinch of salt
- Black pepper to taste

1. Preheat your air fryer to 390°Fahrenheit. Add all the ingredients into a bowl. Place ingredients in a heat safe dish and cook for 20-minutes. Serve warm.

PER SERVING

Calories: 296 | Total Fat: 12.2g | Carbs: 11.8g | Protein: 16.3g

Baked Beef Bowl

Prep Time: 10 minutes | Cook Time: 50 minutes | Serves 2

- 1-pound beef sirloin, chopped
- 1 teaspoon ground nutmeg
- 1 teaspoon salt
- 1 cup radish, chopped
- 1 tablespoon avocado oil
- ½ teaspoon dried basil
- ¼ cup of water

1. Put all ingredients in the air fryer basket and carefully mix.
2. Cook the beef meal at 355F for 50 minutes.

PER SERVING

Calories: 446 | Fat: 15.5g | Fiber: 1.5g | Carbs: 2.9g | Protein: 69.4g

Beef Roast

Prep Time: 5 minutes | Cook Time: 30 minutes | Serves 4

- 2-pounds beef roast, roughly chopped
- 1 teaspoon ground black pepper
- 1 teaspoon minced garlic
- 2 tablespoons avocado oil
- 1 teaspoon dried oregano
- ½ teaspoon cayenne pepper

1. Rub the beef roast with ground black pepper, minced garlic, avocado oil, dried oregano, and cayenne pepper.
2. Put the beef in the air fryer basket and cook at 365F for 30 minutes.

PER SERVING

Calories: 435 | Fat: 15.1g | Fiber: 0.7g | Carbs: 1.3g | Protein: 69.1g

Beef & Mushrooms

Prep Time: 2 minutes | Cook Time: 10 minutes | Serves 1

- 6-ounces of beef
- ¼ onion, diced
- 2 tablespoons of favorite marinade
- ½ cup mushroom slices

1. Cut beef strips or cubes and place in a bowl. Coat the meat with marinade and cover bowl. Place in the fridge for about 3-hours.
2. Put the meat into a baking dish and add onion and mushrooms. Air fry at 350°Fahrenheit for 10-minutes. Serve warm.

PER SERVING

Calories: 296 | Total Fat: 12.4g | Carbs: 11.3g | Protein: 16.2g

Hearty Pork Stew

Prep Time: 10 minutes | Cook Time: 1 hour | Serves 4

- 2 tablespoons olive oil
- 2 pounds pork stew meat
- 1 yellow onion, chopped
- 2 garlic cloves, minced
- 1/4 cup dry sherry wine
- 4 cups chicken bone broth
- 1 cup tomatoes, pureed
- 1 bay laurel
- Sea salt and ground black pepper, to taste
- 2 tablespoons fresh cilantro, chopped

1. Heat the olive oil in a soup pot over a moderate flame. Sear the pork for about 5 minutes, stirring continuously to ensure even cooking; reserve.
2. Cook the yellow onion in the pan drippings until just tender and translucent. Stir in the garlic and continue to sauté for a further 30 seconds.
3. Pour in a splash of dry sherry to deglaze the pan.
4. Pour in the chicken bone broth and bring to a boil. Stir in the tomatoes and bay laurel. Season with salt and pepper to taste. Turn the heat to medium-low and continue to cook 10 minutes longer.
5. Add the reserved pork back to the pot, partially cover, and continue to simmer for 45
6. minutes longer. Garnish with cilantro and serve hot. Bon appétit!

PER SERVING

Calories: 332 | Fat: 14.7g | Carbs: 3.9g | Protein: 41g | Fiber: 0.8g

Fast Mongolian Beef

Prep Time: 15 minutes | Cook Time: 20 minutes | Serves 2

- 10 oz beef steak, chopped
- 2 tablespoons almond flour
- 1 teaspoon avocado oil
- ½ teaspoon onion powder
- 4 tablespoons coconut aminos
- 1 teaspoon Erythritol

1. Mix the beef steak with onion powder, coconut aminos, and Erythritol.
2. Then coat every beef steak piece with almond flour and put in the air fryer basket.
3. Sprinkle the beef with avocado oil and cook at 365F for 10 minutes per side.

PER SERVING

Calories: 341 | Fat: 12.5g | Fiber: 0.9g | Carbs: 10.6g | Protein: 44.6g

Rich Bacon and Pork Omelet

Prep Time: 5 minutes | Cook Time: 15 minutes | Serves 5

- 2 ounces bacon, diced
- 1 pound ground pork
- 1 shallot, chopped
- 1 teaspoon ginger-garlic paste
- 6 eggs, whisked

1. Heat up a nonstick skillet over a moderate flame. Now, cook the bacon until it releases easily from the bottom of the skillet.
2. Then, add in the ground pork and shallot and cook for 4 to 5 minutes or until the pork is no longer pink; discard the excess fat.
3. Fold in the ginger-garlic paste and whisked eggs; partially cover and let it cook on mediumlow temperature for 4 minutes. Flip your omelet and cook on the other side for 3 minutes longer.
4. Slide your omelet onto a plate and serve right now. Bon appétit!

PER SERVING

Calories: 393 | Fat: 28g | Carbs: 0.8g | Protein: 31.4g | Fiber: 0.1g

Saucy Pork Cutlets

Prep Time: 5 minutes | **Cook Time:** 25 minutes | **Serves 2**

- 1 tablespoon lard, softened at room temperature
- 2 pork cutlets, 2-inch-thick
- 1/3 cup dry red wine
- 2 garlic cloves, sliced
- 1/2 teaspoon whole black peppercorns
- 4 tablespoons flaky salt
- 1 teaspoon juniper berries
- 1/2 teaspoon cayenne pepper

1. Melt the lard in a nonstick skillet over a moderate flame. Now, brown the pork cutlets for about 8 minutes, turning them over to ensure even cooking; reserve.
2. Add a splash of wine to deglaze the pan. Stir in the remaining ingredients and continue to cook until fragrant or for a minute or so.
3. Return the pork cutlets to the skillet, continue to cook until the sauce has thickened and everything is heated through about 10 minutes. Serve warm. Bon appétit!

PER SERVING

Calories: 369 | Fat: 20.6g | Carbs: 1.1g | Protein: 40.1g | Fiber: 0.1g

Simple and Delicious Chili Con Carne

Prep Time: 10 minutes | **Cook Time:** 50 minutes | **Serves 4**

- 2 ounces bacon, diced
- 1 red onion, chopped
- 1 pound ground pork
- 1 teaspoon ground cumin
- 2 cloves garlic, minced
- 1 teaspoon chipotle powder
- Kosher salt and ground black pepper, to taste
- 1/2 cup beef broth
- 2 ripe tomatoes, crushed

1. Heat up a medium stockpot over a moderate flame. Cook the bacon until crisp; reserve.
2. Cook the onion and ground pork in the bacon grease. Cook until the ground pork is no longer pink and the onion just begins to brown.
3. Stir in the ground cumin and garlic and continue to sauté for 30 seconds more or until aromatic.
4. Add the chipotle powder, salt, black pepper, broth, and tomatoes to the pot. Cook, partially covered, for 45 minutes or until heated through.
5. You can add 1/4 cup of water during the cooking, as needed. Serve with the reserved bacon and other favorite toppings. Enjoy!

PER SERVING

Calories: 389 | Fat: 29.9g | Carbs: 5.3g | Protein: 22.2g | Fiber: 1.6g

Chapter 7
Fish and Seafood

Kataifi-Wrapped Shrimp with Lemon Garlic Butter

Prep Time: 5 minutes | Cook Time: 22 minutes | Serves 5

- 20 large green shrimps,
- peeled and deveined
- 7 tablespoons unsalted butter
- 12-ounces of kataifi pastry
- Wedges of lemon or lime
- Salt and pepper to taste
- 5 cloves of garlic, crushed
- 2 lemons, zested and juiced

1. In a pan, over low heat melt butter. Add the garlic and lemon zest, and sauté for about 2-minutes. Season with salt, pepper and lemon juice. Cover the shrimp with half of garlic butter sauce and set aside remaining half of sauce.
2. Preheat your air fryer to 360°Fahrenheit and cover the tray with a sheet of foil. Remove the pastry from the bag and tease out strands. On the countertop lay 6-inch strands. Roll shrimp and butter into pastry. Shrimp tail should be exposed. Repeat process for all shrimp.
3. Place the shrimp into air fryer for 10-minutes. Flip shrimp over and place back into air fryer for another 10-minutes. Serve with a salad and lime or lemon wedges. Dip the shrimp into remaining garlic butter sauce.

PER SERVING

Calories: 301 | Total Fat: 10.3g | Carbs: 9.5g | Protein: 15.4g

---

Fish Taco

Prep Time: 5 minutes | Cook Time: 8 minutes | Serves 2

- 1½ cups almond flour
- 1 can of beer
- 1 teaspoon baking powder
- 1 teaspoon sea salt
- ½ cup salsa
- 8-ounces fresh halibut, sliced into small strips
- Corn tortillas
- Cilantro, chopped
- Cholula sauce to taste
- 2 tablespoons olive oil
- 2 chili peppers, sliced
- 1 large avocado
- ¾ cup buttermilk
- ½ lime juiced

1. Make your batter by mixing baking powder, 1 cup of flour, beer, and salt. Stir well. Cover the halibut with remaining ½ cup of flour and dip it into the batter to coat well. Preheat your air fryer to 390°Fahrenheit and grease air fry basket with olive oil. Cook the fish for 8-minutes.
2. Mix the avocado cream ingredients in a blender until smooth. Place the corn tortillas on a plate and cover with salsa. Set aside. Put the fish on top of tortillas and cover with avocado cream. Add Cholula sauce, sprinkle with cilantro and top with chili slices and serve.

PER SERVING

Calories: 302 | Total Fat: 9.2g | Carbs: 8.7g | Protein: 15.2g

---

Grilled Barramundi with Lemon Butter

Prep Time: 10 minutes | Cook Time: 40 minutes | Serves 2

- 1 lb. small potatoes
- 7-ounces barramundi fillets
- 1 teaspoon olive oil
- ¼ bunch of fresh thyme, chopped
- Green beans, cooked, optional
- 1 scallion, chopped
- ½ cup thickened cream
- ½ cup white wine
- 1 bay leaf
- 10 black peppercorns
- 1 clove garlic, chopped
- 8-ounces unsalted butter
- 1 lemon, juiced
- Salt and pepper to taste

1. Preheat your air fryer to 390°Fahrenheit for 5-minutes. In a bowl, add potatoes, salt, thyme and olive oil. Mix ingredients well. Put potatoes into air fryer basket and cook for 20-minutes. Layer the fish fillets in a basket on top of potatoes. Cook for another 20-minutes. Prepare the sauce on top of the stove. Heat scallion and garlic over medium-high heat and add the peppercorns and bay leaf. Pour in the wine and reduce heat to low.
2. Add the thickened cream and stir to blend. Add the butter and whisk over low heat. When butter has melted add salt, pepper, and lemon juice. Strain the sauce to remove peppercorns and bay leaf. Place the fish and potatoes on serving plate and add sauce and serve with green beans.

PER SERVING

Calories: 302 | Total Fat: 9.6g | Carbs: 8.3g | Protein: 15.8g

Ginger Cod

Prep Time: 10 minutes | Cook Time: 8 minutes | Serves 2

- 10 oz cod fillet
- ½ teaspoon cayenne pepper
- ¼ teaspoon ground coriander
- ½ teaspoon ground ginger
- ½ teaspoon ground black pepper
- 1 tablespoon sunflower oil
- ½ teaspoon salt
- ½ teaspoon dried rosemary
- ½ teaspoon ground paprika

1. In the shallow bowl mix up cayenne pepper, ground coriander, ginger, ground black pepper, salt, dried rosemary, and ground paprika. Then rub the cod fillet with the spice mixture. After this, sprinkle it with sunflower oil.
2. Preheat the air fryer to 390F. Place the cod fillet in the air fryer and cook it for 4 minutes. Then carefully flip the fish on another side and cook for 4 minutes more.

PER SERVING

Calories: 183 | Fat: 8.5g | Fiber: 0.7g | Carbs: 1.4g | Protein: 25.6g

Paprika Tilapia

Prep Time: 5 minutes | Cook Time: 20 minutes | Serves 4

- 4 tilapia fillets, boneless
- 3 tablespoons ghee, melted
- A pinch of salt and black pepper
- 2 tablespoons capers
- 1 teaspoon garlic powder
- ½ teaspoon smoked paprika
- ½ teaspoon oregano, dried
- 2 tablespoons lemon juice

1. In a bowl, mix all the ingredients except the fish and toss. Arrange the fish in a pan that fits the air fryer, pour the capers mix all over, put the pan in the air fryer and cook 360 degrees F for 20 minutes, shaking halfway. Divide between plates and serve hot.

PER SERVING

Calories: 224 | Fat: 10g | Fiber: 0g | Carbs: 2g | Protein: 18g

Butter Crab Muffins

Prep Time: 15 minutes | Cook Time: 20 minutes | Serves 2

- 5 oz crab meat, chopped
- 2 eggs, beaten
- 2 tablespoons almond flour
- ¼ teaspoon baking powder
- ½ teaspoon apple cider vinegar
- ½ teaspoon ground paprika
- 1 tablespoon butter, softened
- Cooking spray

1. Grind the chopped crab meat and put it in the bowl. Add eggs, almond flour, baking powder, apple cider vinegar, ground paprika, and butter. Stir the mixture until homogenous.
2. Preheat the air fryer to 365F. Spray the muffin molds with cooking spray. Then pour the crab meat batter in the muffin molds and place them in the preheated air fryer. Cook the crab muffins for 20 minutes or until they are light brown.
3. Cool the cooked muffins to the room temperature and remove from the muffin mold.

PER SERVING

Calories: 340 | Fat: 25.5g | Fiber: 3.2g | Carbs: 8.2g | Protein: 20.5g

Cranberry Cod

Prep Time: 5 minutes | Cook Time: 20 minutes | Serves 2

- 3 filets cod
- 1 tablespoon olive oil
- 3 tablespoons cranberry jam

1. Preheat your air fryer to 390°Fahrenheit. Brush the cod filets with olive oil. Spoon a tablespoon of cranberry jam on each filet. Cook for 20-minutes.

PER SERVING

Calories: 289 | Total Fat: 9.2g | Carbs: 8.3g | Protein: 14.3g

Shrimp Skewers

Prep Time: 10 minutes | Cook Time: 5 minutes | Serves 5

- 4-pounds shrimps, peeled
- 2 tablespoons fresh cilantro, chopped
- 2 tablespoons apple cider vinegar
- 1 teaspoon ground coriander
- 1 tablespoon avocado oil
- Cooking spray

1. In the shallow bowl mix up avocado oil, ground coriander, apple cider vinegar, and fresh cilantro. Then put the shrimps in the big bowl and sprinkle with avocado oil mixture. Mix them well and leave for 10 minutes to marinate.
2. After this, string the shrimps on the skewers. Preheat the air fryer to 400F. Arrange the shrimp skewers in the air fryer and cook them for 5 minutes.

PER SERVING

Calories: 223 | Fat: 14.9g | Fiber: 3.1g | Carbs: 5.5g | Protein: 17.4g

Cod Fish Teriyaki with Oysters, Mushrooms & Veggies

Prep Time: 5 minutes | Cook Time: 10 minutes | Serves 2

- 1 tablespoon olive oil
- 6 pieces mini king oyster
- mushrooms, thinly sliced
- 2 slices (1-inch) codfish
- 1 Napa cabbage leaf, sliced
- 1 clove garlic, chopped
- Salt to taste
- 1 green onion, minced
- Veggies, steamed of your choice
- 1 teaspoon liquid stevia
- 2 tablespoons mirin
- 2 tablespoons soy sauce

1. Prepare teriyaki sauce by mixing all the ingredients in a bowl then set aside. Grease the air fryer basket with oil. Place the mushrooms, garlic, Napa cabbage leaf, and salt inside. Layer the fish on top.
2. Preheat your air fryer to 360°Fahrenheit for 3-minutes. Place the basket in air fryer and cook for 5-minutes. Stir. Pour the teriyaki sauce over ingredients in the basket. Cook for an additional 5-minutes. Serve with your choice of steamed veggies.

PER SERVING

Calories: 297 | Total Fat: 10.6g | Carbs: 9.2g | Protein: 14.2g

Stevia Cod

Prep Time: 5 minutes | Cook Time: 14 minutes | Serves 4

- 1/3 cup stevia
- 2 tablespoons coconut aminos
- 4 cod fillets, boneless
- A pinch of salt and black pepper

1. In a pan that fits the air fryer, combine all the ingredients and toss gently. Introduce the pan in the fryer and cook at 350 degrees F for 14 minutes, flipping the fish halfway. Divide everything between plates and serve.

PER SERVING

Calories: 267 | Fat: 18g | Fiber: 2g | Carbs: 5g | Protein: 20g

Onion Shrimps

Prep Time: 10 minutes | Cook Time: 5 minutes | Serves 3

- pound shrimps, peeled
- 1 teaspoon onion powder
- 1 teaspoon avocado oil
- ½ teaspoon salt

1. Sprinkle the shrimps with onion powder, avocado oil, and salt.
2. Put the shrimps in the air fryer and cook at 400F for 5 minutes.

PER SERVING

Calories: 185 | Fat: 2.8g | Fiber: 0.1g | Carbs: 3g | Protein: 34.5g

Balsamic Tilapia

Prep Time: 5 minutes | Cook Time: 15 minutes | Serves 4

- 4 tilapia fillets, boneless
- 2 tablespoons balsamic vinegar
- 1 teaspoon avocado oil
- 1 teaspoon dried basil

1. Sprinkle the tilapia fillets with balsamic vinegar, avocado oil, and dried basil.
2. Then put the fillets in the air fryer basket and cook at 365F for 15 minutes.

PER SERVING

Calories: 96 | Fat: 1.2g | Fiber: 0.1g | Carbs: 0.2g | Protein: 21g

Crunchy Red Fish

Prep Time: 15 minutes | Cook Time: 8 minutes | Serves 4

- 2-pound salmon fillet
- ¼ cup coconut shred
- 2 eggs, beaten
- 1 teaspoon coconut oil
- 1 teaspoon Italian seasonings

1. Cut the salmon fillet into servings.
2. Then sprinkle the fish with Italian seasonings and dip in the eggs.
3. After this, coat every salmon fillet in coconut shred and put it in the air fryer.
4. Cook the fish at 375F for 4 minutes per side.

PER SERVING

Calories: 395 | Fat: 22.7g | Fiber: 1g | Carbs: 2.3g | Protein: 46.8

Chapter 8
Vegetarian Recipes

Croissant Mushroom & Egg

Prep Time: 5 minutes | Cook Time: 8 minutes | Serves 1

- 1 croissant, sliced in half crosswise
- ½ sprig rosemary, chopped
- 1 large egg
- Salt and pepper to taste
- 3 cherry tomatoes, halved
- 1 ½ ounces of cheddar cheese, shredded
- 4 small button mushrooms, quartered
- Handful of salad greens
- Butter for greasing baking dish

1. Prepare baking dish by greasing it with butter. Arrange all the ingredients in two layers in baking dish except for salad greens and croissant. Crack egg into baking dish, add mushrooms and cheese on the top then season with salt, pepper, and rosemary.
2. Preheat your air fryer to 325°Fahrenheit. Bake for 8-minutes and then assemble your breakfast sandwich and enjoy!

PER SERVING

Calories: 223 | Total Fat: 10.2g | Carbs: 9.4g | Protein: 14.3g

Mushroom, Onion and Feta Frittata

Prep Time: 10 minutes | Cook Time: 30 minutes | Serves 4

- 4 cups button mushrooms
- 1 red onion
- 2 tablespoons olive oil
- 6 tablespoons feta cheese, crumbled
- Pinch of salt
- 6 eggs
- Cooking spray

1. Peel and slice the red onion into ¼ inch thin slices. Clean the button mushrooms, then cut them into ¼ inch thin slices. Add olive oil to pan and sauté mushrooms over medium heat until tender. Remove from heat and pan so that they can cool.
2. Preheat your air fryer to 330°Fahrenheit. Add cracked eggs into a bowl, and whisk them, adding a pinch of salt. Coat an 8-inch heat resistant baking dish with cooking spray. Add the eggs into the baking dish, then onion and mushroom mixture, and then add feta cheese. Place the baking dish into air fryer for 30-minutes and serve warm.

PER SERVING

Calories: 246 | Total Fat: 12.3g | Carbs: 9.2g | Protein: 10.3g

Lemon Asparagus

Prep Time: 5 minutes | Cook Time: 12 minutes | Serves 4

- 1 pound asparagus, trimmed
- A pinch of salt and black pepper
- 2 tablespoons olive oil
- 3 garlic cloves, minced
- 3 tablespoons parmesan, grated
- Juice of 1 lemon

1. In a bowl, mix the asparagus with the rest of the ingredients and toss. Put the asparagus in your air fryer's basket and cook at 390 degrees F for 12 minutes. Divide between plates and serve.

PER SERVING

Calories: 175 | Fat: 5g | Fiber: 2g | Carbs: 4g | Protein: 8g

Bacon, Lettuce, Tempeh & Tomato Sandwiches

Prep Time: 3 minutes | Cook Time: 5 minutes | Serves 4

- 8-ounce package tempeh
- 1 cup warm vegetable broth
- Tomato slices and lettuce, to serve
- ¼ teaspoon chipotle chili powder
- ½ teaspoon garlic powder
- ½ teaspoon onion powder
- 1 teaspoon Liquid smoke
- 3 tablespoons soy sauce

1. Begin by opening the packet of tempeh and slice into pieces about ¼ inch thick. Grab a medium bowl and add the remaining ingredients except for lettuce and tomato and stir well. Place the pieces of tempeh onto a baking tray that will fit into your air fryer and pour over the flavor mix.
2. Put the tray in air fryer and cook for 5-minutes at 360°Fahrenheit. Remove from air fryer and place on sliced bread with the tomato and lettuce and any other extra toppings you desire.

PER SERVING

Carbs: 265 | Total Fat: 11.3g | Carbs: 9.2g | Protein: 12.4g

Curried Cauliflower Florets
Prep Time: 5 minutes | **Cook Time:** 10 minutes | **Serves 4**

- 1/4 cup sultanas or golden raisins
- ¼ teaspoon salt
- 1 tablespoon curry powder
- 1 head cauliflower, broken into small florets
- ¼ cup pine nuts
- ½ cup olive oil

1. In a cup of boiling water, soak your sultanas to plump. Preheat your air fryer to 350°Fahrenheit. Add oil and pine nuts to air fryer and toast for a minute or so.
2. In a bowl toss the cauliflower and curry powder as well as salt, then add the mix to air fryer mixing well. Cook for 10-minutes. Drain the sultanas, toss with cauliflower, and serve.

PER SERVING
Calories: 275 | Total Fat: 11.3g | Carbs: 8.6g | Protein: 9.5g

Mustard Garlic Asparagus
Prep Time: 5 minutes | **Cook Time:** 12 minutes | **Serves 4**

- 1 pound asparagus, trimmed
- 2 tablespoons olive oil
- ¼ cup mustard
- 3 garlic cloves, minced
- ½ cup parmesan, grated

1. In a bowl, mix the asparagus with the oil, garlic and mustard and toss really well. Put the asparagus spears in your air fryer's basket and cook at 400 degrees F for 12 minutes. Divide between plates, sprinkle the parmesan on top and serve.

PER SERVING
Calories: 162 | Fat: 4g | Fiber: 4g | Carbs: 6g | Protein: 9g

Nutmeg Okra
Prep Time: 10 minutes | **Cook Time:** 10 minutes | **Serves 4**

- pound okra, trimmed
- 3 oz pancetta, sliced
- ½ teaspoon ground nutmeg
- ½ teaspoon salt
- 1 teaspoon sunflower oil

1. Sprinkle okra with ground nutmeg and salt. Then put the vegetables in the air fryer and sprinkle with sunflower. Chop pancetta roughly. Top the okra with pancetta and cook the meal for 10 minutes at 360F.

PER SERVING
Calories: 172 | Fat: 10.4g | Fiber: 3.7g | Carbs: 8.9g | Protein: 10.1g

Parsnip Fries
Prep Time: 5 minutes | **Cook Time:** 12 minutes | **Serves 2**

- 2 tablespoons of olive oil
- A pinch of sea salt
- 1 large bunch of parsnips

1. Wash and peel the parsnips, then cut them into strips. Place the parsnips in a bowl with the olive oil and sea salt and coat well.
2. Preheat your air fryer to 360°Fahrenheit. Place the parsnip and oil mixture into the air fryer basket. Cook for 12-minutes. Serve with sour cream or ketchup.

PER SERVING
Calories: 262g | Total Fat: 11.3g | Carbs: 10.4g | Protein: 7.2g

Feta Peppers
Prep Time: 15 minutes | **Cook Time:** 10 minutes | **Serves 4**

- 5 oz Feta, crumbled
- 8 oz banana pepper, trimmed
- 1 teaspoon sesame oil
- 1 garlic clove, minced
- ½ teaspoon fresh dill, chopped
- 1 teaspoon lemon juice
- ½ teaspoon lime zest, grated

1. Clean the seeds from the peppers and cut them into halves. Then sprinkle the peppers with sesame oil and put in the air fryer. Cook them for 10 minutes at 385F. Flip the peppers on another side after 5 minutes of cooking.
2. Meanwhile, mix up minced garlic, fresh dill, lemon juice, and lime zest. Put the cooked banana peppers on the plate and sprinkle with lemon juice mixture. Then top the vegetables with crumbled feta.

PER SERVING
Calories: 107 | Fat: 8.7g | Fiber: 0.2g | Carbs: 2.2g | Protein: 5.2g

Sesame Fennel
Prep Time: 10 minutes | **Cook Time:** 15 minutes | **Serves 2**

- 8 oz fennel bulb
- 1 teaspoon sesame oil
- ½ teaspoon salt
- 1 teaspoon white pepper

1. Trim the fennel bulb and cut it into halves. Then sprinkle the fennel bulb with salt, white pepper, and sesame oil.
2. Preheat the air fryer to 370F. Put the fennel bulb halves in the air fryer and cook them for 15 minutes.

PER SERVING
Calories: 58 | Fat: 2.5g | Fiber: 3.8g | Carbs: 9g | Protein: 1.5g

Swiss Chard Patties

Prep Time: 15 minutes | Cook Time: 6 minutes | Serves 2

- 1 cup swiss chard, chopped
- 1 zucchini, grated
- 2 tablespoons almond flour
- 1 egg, beaten
- 1 teaspoon olive oil
- 1 teaspoon salt

1. In the mixing bowl, mix swiss chard with zucchini, almond flour, egg, and salt.
2. Make the patties from the mixture.
3. Then brush the air fryer basket with olive oil from inside and put the patties there.
4. Cook the meal at 400F for 3 minutes per side.

PER SERVING

Calories: 113 | Fat: 8.1g | Fiber: 2.1g | Carbs: 5.6g | Protein: 5.8g

Bacon Asparagus

Prep Time: 5 minutes | Cook Time: 10 minutes | Serves 4

- 1-pound asparagus, trimmed
- 2 oz bacon, sliced
- 1 teaspoon avocado oil
- ½ teaspoon salt

1. Wrap the asparagus in the bacon slices and sprinkle with avocado oil and salt.
2. Put the vegetables in the air fryer and cook at 400F for 10 minutes.

PER SERVING

Calories: 101 | Fat: 6.2g | Fiber: 2.4g | Carbs: 4.7g | Protein: 7.8g

Snap Peas Mash

Prep Time: 10 minutes | Cook Time: 6 minutes | Serves 4

- 1 cup snap peas, frozen
- 2 oz Provolone, shredded
- 1 teaspoon coconut oil
- ½ teaspoon chili powder
- ¼ cup chicken stock

1. Mix snap peas with coconut oil and chicken stock and put in the air fryer.
2. Cook them for 6 minutes at 400F.
3. After this, transfer the snap peas in the blender, add all remaining ingredients and blend until smooth.

PER SERVING

Calories: 90 | Fat: 5.2g | Fiber: 2g | Carbs: 5.8g | Protein: 5.7g

Chapter 9
Desserts and Staples

Country-Style Coconut & Macadamia Cookies

Prep Time: 15 minutes | Cook Time: 25 minutes | Serves 10

- ¾ cup coconut oil, room temperature
- 1 ½ cups coconut flour
- 1 ¼ cups macadamia nuts, unsalted and chopped
- ½ teaspoon pure vanilla extract
- 1/3 teaspoon baking soda
- ½ teaspoon baking powder
- 1/3 teaspoon cloves, ground
- ¼ teaspoon nutmeg, freshly grated
- 2 tablespoons Truvia for baking
- 2 cups almond flour
- 3 eggs plus and egg yolk, whisked
- ½ teaspoon pure coconut extract
- 1/8 teaspoon fine sea salt

1. In a bowl, combine both types of flour, baking soda and baking powder. In another bowl, beat the eggs with coconut oil. Combine the egg mixture with the flour mixture. Add other ingredients and shape into cookies. Bake at 370°Fahrenheit for 25-minutes.

PER SERVING

Calories: 492 | Total Fat: 36.2g | Carbs: 34.8g | Protein: 11.1g

Almond Butter Cookies

Prep Time: 5 minutes | Cook Time: 13 minutes | Serves 8

- ½ cup slivered almonds
- 1 stick butter, room temperature
- 2 tablespoons Truvia
- 1/3 cup almond flour
- 1/3 cup coconut flour
- 1/3 teaspoons ground cloves
- 1 tablespoon candied ginger
- ¾ teaspoon pure vanilla extract

1. In a mixing dish, beat Truvia, butter, vanilla extract, ground cloves, and ginger until light and fluffy. Then, throw in the both kinds of flour and slivered almonds. Continue to mix until a soft dough is formed. Cover and place into fridge for 35-minutes. Preheat your air-fryer to 315°Fahrenheit.
2. Roll the dough into small cookies and place them on the air-fryer cake pan; gently press each cookie using the back of a spoon. Bake cookies for 13-minutes.

PER SERVING

Calories: 252 | Total Fat: 16.2g | Carbs: 25.1g | Protein: 3.3g

Chocolate Raspberry Cake

Prep Time: 5 minutes | Cook Time: 20 minutes | Serves 4

- 1/8 teaspoon fine sea salt
- 1 tablespoon candied ginger
- ½ teaspoon ground cinnamon
- 2 tablespoons cocoa powder
- 3-ounces almond flour
- 1 egg plus 1 egg white, lightly whisked
- ¼ cup unsalted butter, room temperature
- 2 tablespoons Truvia for baking
- 6-ounces raspberries, fresh
- 1 tablespoon Truvia
- 1 teaspoon lime juice, fresh

1. Preheat your air-fryer to 315°Fahrenheit. Then, spritz the inside of two cakes pans with buttered-flavored cooking spray. In a mixing bowl, beat Truvia and butter until creamy. Then, stir in the whisked eggs. Stir in the cocoa powder, flour, cinnamon, ginger and salt. Press the batter dividing it evenly into cake pans; use a wide spatula to level the surface of batter. Bake for 20-minutes.
2. While your cake is baking, stir together the ingredients for filling in a saucepan. Cook over high heat, stirring often and mashing; bring to a boil and decrease the temperature. Cook for about 7-minutes or until mixture thickens. Allow filling to cool at room temperature.
3. Spread half of raspberry filling over first cake, then top with other cake and spread the remaining raspberry filling on top.

PER SERVING

Calories: 331 | Total Fat: 14.9g | Carbs: 47.6g | Protein: 26.9g

Lemon Zucchini Bread

Prep Time: 10 minutes | Cook Time: 40 minutes | Serves 12

- 2 cups almond flour
- 2 teaspoons baking powder
- ¾ cup swerve
- ½ cup coconut oil, melted
- 1 teaspoon lemon juice
- 1 teaspoon vanilla extract
- 3 eggs, whisked
- 1 cup zucchini, shredded
- 1 tablespoon lemon zest
- Cooking spray

1. In a bowl, mix all the ingredients except the cooking spray and stir well. Grease a loaf pan that fits the air fryer with the cooking spray, line with parchment paper and pour the loaf mix inside.
2. Put the pan in the air fryer and cook at 330 degrees F for 40 minutes. Cool down, slice and serve.

PER SERVING

Calories: 143 | Fat: 11g | Fiber: 1g | Carbs: 3g | Protein: 3g

Orange Muffins

Prep Time: 10 minutes | Cook Time: 10 minutes | Serves 5

- 5 eggs, beaten
- 1 tablespoon poppy seeds
- 1 teaspoon vanilla extract
- ¼ teaspoon ground nutmeg
- ½ teaspoon baking powder
- 1 teaspoon orange juice
- 1 teaspoon orange zest, grated
- 5 tablespoons coconut flour
- 1 tablespoon Monk fruit
- 2 tablespoons coconut flakes
- Cooking spray

1. In the mixing bowl mix up eggs, poppy seeds, vanilla extract, ground nutmeg, baking powder, orange juice, orange zest, coconut flour, and Monk fruit. Add coconut flakes and mix up the mixture until it is homogenous and without any clumps.
2. Preheat the air fryer to 360F. Spray the muffin molds with cooking spray from inside. Pour the muffin batter in the molds and transfer them in the air fryer. Cook the muffins for 10 minutes.

PER SERVING

Calories: 119 | Fat: 7.1g | Fiber: 3.4g | Carbs: 6.2g | Protein: 7.5g

Tender Macadamia Bars

Prep Time: 15 minutes | Cook Time: 30 minutes | Serves 10

- 3 tablespoons butter, softened
- 1 teaspoon baking powder
- 1 teaspoon apple cider vinegar
- 1.5 cup coconut flour
- 3 tablespoons swerve
- 1 teaspoon vanilla extract
- 2 eggs, beaten
- 2 oz macadamia nuts, chopped
- Cooking spray

1. Spray the air fryer basket with cooking spray.
2. Then mix all remaining ingredients in the mixing bowl and stir until you get a homogenous mixture.
3. Pour the mixture in the air fryer basket and cook at 345F for 30 minutes.
4. When the mixture is cooked, cut it into bars and transfer in the serving plates

PER SERVING

Calories: 158 | Fat: 10.4g | Fiber: 7.7g | Carbs: 13.1g | Protein: 4g

Lemon Pie

Prep Time: 10 minutes | Cook Time: 35 minutes | Serves 8

- 2 eggs, whisked
- ¾ cup swerve
- ¼ cup coconut flour
- 2 tablespoons butter, melted
- 1 teaspoon lemon zest, grated
- 1 teaspoon baking powder
- 1 teaspoon vanilla extract
- ½ teaspoon lemon extract
- 4 ounces coconut, shredded
- Cooking spray

1. In a bowl, combine all the ingredients except the cooking spray and stir well. Grease a pie pan that fits the air fryer with the cooking spray, pour the mixture inside, put the pan in the air fryer and cook at 360 degrees F for 35 minutes.
2. Slice and serve warm.

PER SERVING

Calories: 212 | Fat: 15g | Fiber: 2g | Carbs: 6g | Protein: 4g

Raisin Muffins

Prep Time: 5 minutes | Cook Time: 15 minutes | Serves 6

- ¼ teaspoon salt
- ½ teaspoon lemon zest, grated
- 1/3 teaspoon ground anise star
- 1/3 teaspoon allspice, ground
- 2 eggs
- 2 cups almond flour
- 1 ¼ teaspoons baking powder
- 1 cup sour cream
- ½ cup coconut oil
- 2 tablespoons Truvia for baking
- ¾ cup raisins

1. In a bowl, combine flour, baking powder, Truvia, salt, star anise, allspice and lemon zest. In another bowl, whisk coconut oil, sour cream, eggs, and whisk to combine. Now, add the wet mixture to the dry mixture and fold in the raisins.
2. Press the batter mixture into a lightly greased muffin tin. Bake at 345°Fahrenheit for 15-minutes.

PER SERVING

Calories: 560 | Total Fat: 28.3g | Carbs: 73.4g | Protein: 7.9g

Cinnamon Zucchini Bread

Prep Time: 10 minutes | **Cook Time:** 40 minutes | **Serves 12**

- 2 cups coconut flour
- 2 teaspoons baking powder
- ¾ cup Erythritol
- ½ cup coconut oil, melted
- 1 teaspoon apple cider vinegar
- 1 teaspoon vanilla extract
- 3 eggs, beaten
- 1 zucchini, grated
- 1 teaspoon ground cinnamon

1. In the mixing bowl, mix coconut flour with baking powder, Erythritol, coconut oil, apple cider vinegar, vanilla extract, eggs, zucchini, and ground cinnamon.
2. Transfer the mixture in the air fryer basket and flatten it in the shape of the bread.
3. Cook the bread at 350F for 40 minutes.

PER SERVING

Calories: 179 | Fat: 12.2g | Fiber: 8.3g | Carbs: 14.6g | Protein: 4.3g

Cream Cheese Scones

Prep Time: 20 minutes | **Cook Time:** 10 minutes | **Serves 4**

- 4 oz almond flour
- ½ teaspoon baking powder
- 1 teaspoon lemon juice
- ¼ teaspoon salt
- 2 teaspoons cream cheese
- ¼ cup coconut cream
- 1 teaspoon vanilla extract
- 1 tablespoon Erythritol
- 1 tablespoon heavy cream
- Cooking spray

1. In the mixing bowl mix up almond flour, baking powder, lemon juice, and salt. Add cream cheese and stir the mixture gently. Mix up vanilla extract and coconut cream in the separated bowl. Add the coconut cream mixture in the almond flour mixture. Stir it gently and then knead the dough. Roll up the dough and cut it on squares (scones).
2. Preheat the air fryer to 360F. Spray the air fryer basket with cooking spray and put the scones inside air fryer in one layer. Cook the scones for 10 minutes or until they are light brown. Then cool the scones to the room temperature. Meanwhile, mix up heavy cream and Erythritol. Then brush every scone with a sweet cream mixture.

PER SERVING

Calories: 217 | Fat: 19.6g | Fiber: 3.4g | Carbs: 7.4g | Protein: 6.6g

Bread Pudding with Sultanas

Prep Time: 5 minutes | **Cook Time:** 25 minutes | **Serves 8**

- 1 teaspoon vanilla extract
- 1½ tablespoons coffee liqueur
- 1 loaf stale Italian bread, torn into pieces
- 1/3 cup white chocolate chunks
- 3 eggs, whisked
- ¼ cup Sultanas
- 1 1/3 cup skim milk
- 2 tablespoons Truvia for baking

1. Prepare two mixing bowls. Dump bread pieces into first bowl. In the second bowl, combine the remaining ingredients, except the white chocolate and Sultanas; whisk until smooth.
2. Pour the egg/milk mixture over the bread pieces. Allow to soak for 20-minutes; using a large spatula gently press down. Now, scatter chocolate chunks and Sultanas over the top. Divide the bread pudding between two mini loaf pans. Bake in air-fryer for 25-minutes at 320°Fahrenheit.

PER SERVING

Calories: 283 | Total Fat: 4.7g | Carbs: 51.4g | Protein: 8.3g

Berry Pie

Prep Time: 5 minutes | **Cook Time:** 20 minutes | **Serves 8**

- 5 egg whites
- 1/3 cup swerve
- 1 and ½ cups almond flour
- Zest of 1 lemon, grated
- 1 teaspoon baking powder
- 1 teaspoon vanilla extract
- 1/3 cup butter, melted
- 2 cups strawberries, sliced
- Cooking spray

1. In a bowl, whisk egg whites well. Add the rest of the ingredients except the cooking spray gradually and whisk everything. Grease a tart pan with the cooking spray, and pour the strawberries mix. Put the pan in the air fryer and cook at 370 degrees F for 20 minutes.
2. Cool down, slice and serve.

PER SERVING

Calories: 182 | Fat: 12g | Fiber: 1g | Carbs: 6g | Protein: 5g

Vanilla Scones

Prep Time: 20 minutes | Cook Time: 10 minutes | Serves 6

- 4 oz coconut flour
- ½ teaspoon baking powder
- 1 teaspoon apple cider vinegar
- 2 teaspoons mascarpone
- ¼ cup heavy cream
- 1 teaspoon vanilla extract
- 1 tablespoon Erythritol
- Cooking spray

1. In the mixing bowl, mix coconut flour with baking powder, apple cider vinegar, mascarpone, heavy cream, vanilla extract, and Erythritol.
2. Knead the dough and cut into scones.
3. Then put them in the air fryer basket and sprinkle with cooking spray.
4. Cook the vanilla scones at 365F for 10 minutes.

PER SERVING

Calories: 104 | Fat: 4.1g | Fiber: 8.1g | Carbs: 14g | Protein: 3g

Poppy Seeds Muffins

Prep Time: 10 minutes | Cook Time: 10 minutes | Serves 5

- 5 tablespoons coconut oil, softened
- 1 egg, beaten
- 1 teaspoon vanilla extract
- 1 tablespoon poppy seeds
- 1 teaspoon baking powder
- 2 tablespoons Erythritol
- 1 cup coconut flour

1. In the mixing bowl, mix coconut oil with egg, vanilla extract, poppy seeds, baking powder, Erythritol, and coconut flour.
2. When the mixture is homogenous, pour it in the muffin molds and transfer it in the air fryer basket.
3. Cook the muffins for 10 minutes at 365F.

PER SERVING

Calories: 239 | Fat: 17.7g | Fiber: 9.8g | Carbs: 17.1g | Protein: 4.6g

Almond Pie

Prep Time: 10 minutes | Cook Time: 35 minutes | Serves 8

- 2 eggs, beaten
- ¾ cup Erythritol
- ¼ cup almond flour
- 2 tablespoons coconut oil, melted
- 1 teaspoon lime zest, grated
- 1 teaspoon baking powder
- 1 teaspoon vanilla extract
- ½ teaspoon apple cider vinegar
- 1 oz almonds, chopped

1. Mix all ingredients in the mixing bowl and whisk until smooth.
2. Then pour the mixture in the baking pan and flatten gently.
3. Put the baking pan in the air fryer and cook the pie at 365F for 35 minutes

PER SERVING

Calories: 89 | Fat: 7.9g | Fiber: 0.9g | Carbs: 2g | Protein: 2g

Appendix 1 Measurement Conversion Chart

Volume Equivalents (Dry)	
US STANDARD	**METRIC (APPROXIMATE)**
1/8 teaspoon	0.5 mL
1/4 teaspoon	1 mL
1/2 teaspoon	2 mL
3/4 teaspoon	4 mL
1 teaspoon	5 mL
1 tablespoon	15 mL
1/4 cup	59 mL
1/2 cup	118 mL
3/4 cup	177 mL
1 cup	235 mL
2 cups	475 mL
3 cups	700 mL
4 cups	1 L

Volume Equivalents (Liquid)		
US STANDARD	**US STANDARD (OUNCES)**	**METRIC (APPROXIMATE)**
2 tablespoons	1 fl.oz.	30 mL
1/4 cup	2 fl.oz.	60 mL
1/2 cup	4 fl.oz.	120 mL
1 cup	8 fl.oz.	240 mL
1 1/2 cup	12 fl.oz.	355 mL
2 cups or 1 pint	16 fl.oz.	475 mL
4 cups or 1 quart	32 fl.oz.	1 L
1 gallon	128 fl.oz.	4 L

Temperatures Equivalents	
FAHRENHEIT(F)	**CELSIUS(C) APPROXIMATE)**
225 °F	107 °C
250 °F	120 ° °C
275 °F	135 °C
300 °F	150 °C
325 °F	160 °C
350 °F	180 °C
375 °F	190 °C
400 °F	205 °C
425 °F	220 °C
450 °F	235 °C
475 °F	245 °C
500 °F	260 °C

Weight Equivalents	
US STANDARD	**METRIC (APPROXIMATE)**
1 ounce	28 g
2 ounces	57 g
5 ounces	142 g
10 ounces	284 g
15 ounces	425 g
16 ounces (1 pound)	455 g
1.5 pounds	680 g
2 pounds	907 g

Appendix 2 The Dirty Dozen and Clean Fifteen

The Environmental Working Group (EWG) is a nonprofit, nonpartisan organization dedicated to protecting human health and the environment Its mission is to empower people to live healthier lives in a healthier environment. This organization publishes an annual list of the twelve kinds of produce, in sequence, that have the highest amount of pesticide residue-the Dirty Dozen-as well as a list of the fifteen kinds ofproduce that have the least amount of pesticide residue-the Clean Fifteen.

THE DIRTY DOZEN	
The 2016 Dirty Dozen includes the following produce. These are considered among the year's most important produce to buy organic:	
Strawberries	Spinach
Apples	Tomatoes
Nectarines	Bell peppers
Peaches	Cherry tomatoes
Celery	Cucumbers
Grapes	Kale/collard greens
Cherries	Hot peppers
The Dirty Dozen list contains two additional itemskale/collard greens and hot peppers-because they tend to contain trace levels of highly hazardous pesticides.	

THE CLEAN FIFTEEN	
The least critical to buy organically are the Clean Fifteen list. The following are on the 2016 list:	
Avocados	Papayas
Corn	Kiw
Pineapples	Eggplant
Cabbage	Honeydew
Sweet peas	Grapefruit
Onions	Cantaloupe
Asparagus	Cauliflower
Mangos	
Some of the sweet corn sold in the United States are made from genetically engineered (GE) seedstock. Buy organic varieties of these crops to avoid GE produce.	

Appendix 3 Index

A

all-purpose flour	50, 53
allspice	15
almond	5, 14
ancho chile	10
ancho chile powder	5
apple	9
apple cider vinegar	9
arugula	51
avocado	11

B

bacon	52
balsamic vinegar	7, 12, 52
basil	5, 8, 11, 13
beet	52
bell pepper	50, 51, 53
black beans	50, 51
broccoli	51, 52, 53
buns	52
butter	50

C

canola oil	50, 51, 52
carrot	52, 53
cauliflower	5, 52
cayenne	5, 52
cayenne pepper	52
Cheddar cheese	52
chicken	6
chili powder	50, 51
chipanle pepper	50
chives	5, 6, 52
cinnamon	15
coconut	6
Colby Jack cheese	51
coriander	52
corn	50, 51
corn kernels	50
cumin	5, 10, 15, 50, 51, 52

D

diced panatoes	50
Dijon mustard	7, 12, 13, 51
dry onion powder	52

E

egg	14, 50, 53
enchilada sauce	51

F

fennel seed	53
flour	50, 53
fresh chives	5, 6, 52
fresh cilantro	52
fresh cilantro leaves	52
fresh dill	5
fresh parsley	6, 52
fresh parsley leaves	52

G

garlic	5, 9, 10, 11, 13, 14, 50, 51, 52, 53
garlic powder	8, 9, 52, 53

H

half-and-half	50
hemp seeds	8
honey	9, 51

I

instant rice	51

K

kale	14
kale leaves	14
ketchup	53
kosher salt	5, 10, 15

L

lemon	5, 6, 14, 51, 53
lemon juice	6, 8, 11, 13, 14, 51
lime	9, 12
lime juice	9, 12
lime zest	9, 12

M

maple syrup	7, 12, 53
Marinara Sauce	5
micro greens	52
milk	5, 50
mixed berries	12
Mozzarella	50, 53
Mozzarella cheese	50, 53
mushroom	51, 52
mustard	51, 53
mustard powder	53

N

nutritional yeast 5

O

olive oil 5, 12, 13, 14, 50, 51, 52, 53
onion 5, 50, 51
onion powder 8
oregano 5, 8, 10, 50

P

panatoes 50, 52
paprika 5, 15, 52
Parmesan cheese 51, 53
parsley 6, 52
pesto 52
pink Himalayan salt 5, 7, 8, 11
pizza dough 50, 53
pizza sauce 50
plain coconut yogurt 6
plain Greek yogurt 5
porcini powder 53
potato 53

R

Ranch dressing 52
raw honey 9, 12, 13
red pepper flakes 5, 8, 14, 15, 51, 53
ricotta cheese 53

S

saffron 52
Serrano pepper 53
sugar 10
summer squash 51

T

tahini 5, 8, 9, 11
thyme 50
toasted almonds 14
tomato 5, 50, 52, 53
turmeric 15

U

unsalted butter 50
unsweetened almond milk 5

V

vegetable broth 50
vegetable stock 51

W

white wine 8, 11
wine vinegar 8, 10, 11

Y

yogurt 5, 6

Z

zucchini 50, 51, 52, 53

GRACE J. SMALLEY

Printed in Great Britain
by Amazon